T0351704

Pearson Edexcel GCSE (9–1)

Physics

Foundation tier

Revision Guide

Series Consultant: Harry Smith

Author: Dr Mike O'Neill

A note from the publisher

In order to ensure that this resource offers high-quality support for the associated Pearson qualification, it has been through a review process by the awarding body. This process confirms that this resource fully covers the teaching and learning content of the specification or part of a specification at which it is aimed. It also confirms that it demonstrates an appropriate balance between the development of subject skills, knowledge and understanding, in addition to preparation for assessment.

Endorsement does not cover any guidance on assessment activities or processes (e.g. practice questions or advice on how to answer assessment questions), included in the resource nor does it prescribe any particular approach to the teaching or delivery of a related course.

While the publishers have made every attempt to ensure that advice on the qualification and its assessment is accurate, the official specification and associated assessment guidance materials are the only authoritative source of information and should always be referred to for definitive guidance.

Pearson examiners have not contributed to any sections in this resource relevant to examination papers for which they have responsibility.

Examiners will not use endorsed resources as a source of material for any assessment set by Pearson.

Endorsement of a resource does not mean that the resource is required to achieve this Pearson qualification, nor does it mean that it is the only suitable material available to support the qualification, and any resource lists produced by the awarding body shall include this and other appropriate resources.

For the full range of Pearson revision titles across KS2, 11+, KS3, GCSE, Functional Skills, AS/A Level and BTEC visit:
www.pearsonschools.co.uk/revise

A small bit of small print

Pearson Edexcel publishes Sample Assessment Material and the Specification on its website. This is the official content and this book should be used in conjunction with it. The worked examples and questions in this book have been written to help you practise the topics in the specification, and to help you prepare for your exams. Remember that the real exam questions may not look like this, and the questions in this book will not appear in your exams.

Contents

- - - - - - - - - - - - - - - - -

A small bit of small print:
Edexcel publishes Sample Assessment Material and the Specification on its website. This is the official content and this book should be used in conjunction with it. The questions in Now try this have been written to help you practise every topic in the book. Remember: the real exam questions may not look like this.

Key concepts

You need to know the SI units of physical quantities, as well as their multiples and sub-multiples, how to convert between units and how to use significant figures and standard form.

Base SI units

There are six main **base SI units** you need to know.

Name	Unit	Abbreviation
length	metre	m
mass	kilogram	kg
time	second	s
current	ampere or amp	A
temperature	kelvin	K
amount of a substance	mole	mol

Derived SI units

There are nine derived SI units you need to know.

Name	Unit	Abbreviation
frequency	hertz	Hz
force	newton	N
energy	joule	J
power	watt	W
pressure	pascal	Pa
electric charge	coulomb	C
electric potential difference	volt	V
electric resistance	ohm	Ω
magnetic flux density	tesla	T

Multiples and sub-multiples

For values of physical quantities, you need to know the values of these multiples or **prefixes**.

10^9 10^8 10^7 10^6 10^5 10^4 10^3 10^2 10^1 10^0 10^{-1} 10^{-2} 10^{-3} 10^{-4} 10^{-5} 10^{-6} 10^{-7} 10^{-8} 10^{-9}

giga-	mega-	kilo-	centi-	milli-	micro-	nano-
prefix G	prefix M	prefix k	prefix c	prefix m	prefix μ	prefix n
× 1 000 000 000	× 1 000 000	× 1000	÷ 100	÷ 1000	÷ 1 000 000	÷ 1 000 000 000
e.g. 5 GHz	e.g. 5 MW	e.g. 2 km	e.g. 8 cm	e.g. 6 mA	e.g. 7 μs	e.g. 2 nm

Significant figures

Significant figures are either non-zero digits (i.e. the digits 1 to 9) or zeroes between non-zero digits.
- The number **543 563** has 6 significant figures.
- The number 0.**23** has two significant figures.
- The number 0.000 000 000 **254** has 3 significant figures. The zeroes before the '2' are not significant figures.
- The number **3034 0000** has 4 significant figures.

The number 30 339 900 rounded to 5 significant figures is 30 340 000.

Standard form

It is useful to write very large and very small numbers in **standard form**.

This is a number between 1 and 10.

This is an integer – a whole number that can be positive or negative.

$$A \times 10^B$$

You also need to be able to convert between units such as kilometres to metres, or hours to seconds.

Now try this

1 State the number of significant figures in each number.
   (a) 4.56   (1 mark)
   (b) 0.000 564 5   (1 mark)
   (c) 3.0046   (1 mark)
2 Convert:
   (a) 12 hours to seconds   (2 marks)
   (b) 64 km/h to m/s   (2 marks)
3 Convert 58.3 MW to watts. Give your answer in standard form.   (2 marks)
4 The diameter of an atom is 0.000 000 000 1 m. Write this in standard form.   (2 marks)

Scalars and vectors

All physical quantities can be described as either a scalar or a vector quantity.

Scalar quantities

Scalar quantities have a size or a magnitude but no specific direction.

Examples include:
- mass
- speed
- distance
- energy
- temperature.

Vector quantities

Vector quantities have a size or magnitude and a specific direction.

Examples include:
- force or weight
- velocity
- displacement
- acceleration
- momentum.

Speed and velocity

The girl is running to the right so she has a velocity of 5 m/s to the right.

5 m/s

5 m/s

Both the girl and the boy are running at 5 m/s. They have the same speed.

The boy is running to the left so he has a velocity of 5 m/s to the left.

If we take 'to the right' as the positive direction, then the girl has a velocity of +5 m/s and the boy has a velocity of −5 m/s.

Speed has a size but velocity has a size AND a direction.

Velocity is speed in a stated direction.

Worked example

(a) Describe the difference between a scalar and a vector. **(2 marks)**

A scalar has a size, whereas a vector has a size and a specific direction.

(b) Describe an example which shows the difference between a scalar and a vector. **(2 marks)**

Speed is a scalar quantity and may have a value of 5 m/s. Velocity may also have a value of 5 m/s but a direction of north.

All vector quantities can be given positive and negative values to show their direction. Examples include:

1. A force of +4 N may be balanced by a force acting in the opposite direction of −4 N.

2. A car that accelerates at a rate of +2 m/s² could decelerate at −2 m/s².

3. If a distance walked to the right of 20 m is a displacement of +20 m, then the same distance walked to the left from the same starting point is a displacement of −20 m.

Now try this

1 State what is meant by
  (a) a scalar quantity **(1 mark)**
  (b) a vector quantity. **(1 mark)**
2 (a) Which of these quantities is a scalar? **(1 mark)**
  ☐ **A** velocity ☐ **B** acceleration ☐ **C** mass ☐ **D** weight
  (b) Which of these quantities is a vector? **(1 mark)**
  ☐ **A** temperature ☐ **B** energy ☐ **C** speed ☐ **D** electric field
3 A boy has a speed of 4 m/s when running. State his (a) speed and (b) velocity when he is running in the opposite direction. **(2 marks)**

Speed, distance and time

Speed is the distance that a moving object covers each second.

Calculating speed

When a body covers the same distance per second throughout its journey, you can use this equation to calculate its speed:

$$\text{speed (m/s)} = \text{change in distance (m)} \div \text{time taken (s)}$$

The greater the change in distance per second, the faster the object is moving.

When the change in distance over a period of time is zero, the speed is zero and the object is stationary.

Average speed

LEARN IT!
IT'S NOT ON THE EQUATIONS LIST

Objects often change speed during a journey, so it is better to use average speed:

$$\text{average speed (m/s)} = \text{total distance travelled (m)} \div \text{total time taken (s)}$$

You can also write this as:

$$\text{distance travelled (m)} = \text{average speed (m/s)} \times \text{time taken (s)}$$

Distance/time graphs

Distance/time graphs have distance on the y-axis and time on the x-axis. The gradient or slope of the graph tells us about the motion of the vehicle.

A — Constant or steady speed

B — Accelerating (speeding up)

C — Decelerating (slowing down)

D — Stationary

Journeys and distance/time graphs

This distance/time graph tells you about a student's journey.

Steep line: the student is moving much faster than before.

Horizontal line: the student is stationary.

Sloping line: shows that the student is moving. The gradient of the line is shallow, showing that the student is moving slowly.

Worked example

(a) Calculate the speed for each part of the journey shown in the graph on the left.
(3 marks)

speed between 0 and 60 s = 80 m ÷ 60 s
= 1.33 m/s

speed between 60 s and 120 s = 0 m ÷ 60 s
= 0 m/s

speed between 120 s and 140 s
= 160 m ÷ 20 s = 8 m/s

(b) Calculate the average speed for the whole journey. **(2 marks)**

average speed = 240 m ÷ 140 s = 1.7 m/s

(c) The student then travels at 4 m/s for 25 seconds. Calculate how far the student travels in this time.

Distance = speed × time = 4 m/s × 25 s
= 100 m

Now try this

1 Calculate the average speed of a motorbike that travels 120 m in 8 s. **(3 marks)**
2 A cyclist rides a bike at an average speed of 9 m/s for 30 seconds. Calculate the distance that the cyclist travels in this time. **(3 marks)**
3 A car accelerates from 0 m/s to 12 m/s in 5 s. Sketch a distance/time graph to show this. **(3 marks)**

3

Equations of motion

You can use equations to work out the velocity and acceleration of moving bodies.

Acceleration

Acceleration is a change in velocity per second. Acceleration is a vector quantity.

$$\text{acceleration (m/s}^2) = \frac{\text{change in velocity (m/s)}}{\text{time taken (s)}}$$

$$a = \frac{(v - u)}{t}$$

 LEARN IT! IT'S NOT ON THE EQUATIONS LIST

- a is the acceleration
- v is the final velocity
- u is the initial velocity
- t is the time taken

Velocity

Velocity is the change in distance per second.

Velocity is a vector quantity.

(final velocity)² − (initial velocity)² = 2 × acceleration × distance

$$v^2 - u^2 = 2 \times a \times x$$

x is the distance travelled.

You can also write this as:

$$v^2 = u^2 + 2ax$$

If a vehicle is said to be 'starting from rest' then its initial velocity, u, will be zero, so the equation simplifies to $v^2 = 2ax$.

Worked example

A cat changes its speed from 2.5 m/s to 10.0 m/s over a period of 3.0 s. Calculate the cat's acceleration. **(3 marks)**

$v = 10$ m/s, $u = 2.5$ m/s, $t = 3$ s, $a = ?$

$a = (v - u) \div t$

$a = (10.0$ m/s $- 2.5$ m/s$) \div 3.0$ s

$a = 7.5$ m/s $\div 3.0$ s

$a = 2.5$ m/s²

Write down all the quantities you know and the one you need to work out. Then decide which equation you need to use.

Watch out! When using this equation, the value for $(v - u)$ may be negative.

Worked example

A motorcyclist passes through green traffic lights with an initial velocity of 4 m/s and then accelerates at a rate of 2.4 m/s², covering a total distance of 200 m. Calculate the final velocity of the motorcycle. **(4 marks)**

Final velocity² = initial velocity² + 2 × acceleration × distance travelled

final velocity² $= (4)^2 + 2 \times 2.4 \times 200$

$= 16 + 960 = 976$

$= \sqrt{976} = 31.2$ m/s

Maths skills When working out x using this equation, you will need to rearrange it. Subtract u^2 from both sides and then divide both sides by $2a$, to give $x = \frac{v^2 - u^2}{2a}$. Substitute the other values and work out the value of x.

Watch out! When you substitute the values for initial velocity, acceleration and distance, you get a value for final velocity². So you need to find the square root of this value to get the value for the final velocity.

Now try this

1 A dog changes its speed from 2 m/s to 8 m/s in 5 s. Calculate the acceleration of the dog. **(3 marks)**

2 A motorcycle changes its speed from 18 m/s to 6 m/s in 4 s. Calculate the acceleration of the motorcycle in this time. **(3 marks)**

3 A car passes through traffic lights with an initial velocity of 5 m/s and accelerates at a rate of 1.6 m/s² over a distance of 180 m. Calculate the final velocity of the car. **(4 marks)**

Velocity/time graphs

Velocity/time graphs show how the velocity of a vehicle changes with time. You can also work out acceleration and distance travelled from the graph.

Interpreting velocity/time graphs

Velocity/time graphs have velocity plotted on the *y*-axis and time plotted on the *x*-axis. The graph shows you how the velocity changes with time.

- The **slope** or **gradient** of the graph tells us the acceleration of the vehicle.
- The **area under the graph** tells us the **distance travelled**.

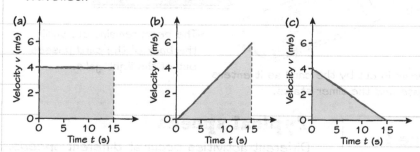

🖩 **Maths skills** Acceleration (gradient) = change in velocity/change in time. For distance travelled (area) use the formulae for the area of a rectangle (base × height, $b \times h$) and area of a triangle ($\frac{1}{2} \times b \times h$). The area will have units of metres, as m/s × s = m.

(a) Acceleration is zero, distance travelled is 60 m.

(b) Acceleration is 0.4 m/s², distance travelled is 45 m.

(c) Acceleration is −0.27 m/s², distance travelled is 30 m.

Velocity/time graphs

This velocity/time graph shows how the velocity of a train along a straight track changes with time.

The train is travelling at a constant velocity.

This is the train's final velocity.

The train is accelerating. The line is steeper than the line between 10 and 30 seconds, so the train's acceleration is greater.

The train is stationary (its velocity is 0).

The sloping line shows that the train is accelerating.

The train is slowing down (its velocity is getting less).

Worked example

Use the velocity/time graph of the train to calculate:
(a) the distance travelled between 10 s and 30 s. **(3 marks)**

Distance travelled is the area of the triangle beneath the line between 10 s and 30 s.

Distance travelled = area
= ½ × (30 − 10)s × 20 m/s = 200 m

(b) the acceleration of the train between 10 s and 30 s. **(3 marks)**

Acceleration = gradient or slope of the line between 10 s and 30 s

= change in velocity ÷ change in time
= (20 − 0) m/s ÷ (30 − 10) s = 1 m/s²

Now try this

1 State what can be determined from the (a) gradient and (b) area beneath a velocity/time graph. **(2 marks)**

2 A car travels a distance of 200 m in 8 s before stopping at traffic lights for 20. It then moves off and travels another 100 m in 5 s. Draw a distance/time graph to show this journey. **(4 marks)**

3 An athlete in a race changes her velocity from 0 m/s to 10 m/s over a time of 4 s. She then runs at a constant velocity of 10 m/s for the next 8 seconds.

(a) Draw a velocity/time graph for this race. **(4 marks)**

(b) Calculate how far she has run in this time. **(3 marks)**

Determining speed

Speed can be determined in the laboratory using light gates and other equipment.

You can measure speeds of objects in the lab by using light gates connected to a computer or data logger.

The speed is found from length of card ÷ time.

card

vehicle

The vehicle is released from its starting position and it moves down the slope.

The light beam is cut by the card as it enters the light gate and the timer starts.

light gate (attached to laptop)

When the card leaves the light gate, the light beam stops the timer.

00:00:00

The beam remains cut until the back of the card passes out of the light gate.

Speed and average speed

The **speed** of an object is how fast it is moving at a given point in time. For example, the speedometer on a car tells the driver the speed at that point in time.

The speed of a car may change regularly over a journey. You can calculate the **average speed** which is the total distance travelled divided by the total time taken to cover that distance.

Typical speeds

Different activities occur at different speeds.

Activity	Typical speed
walking	1.5 m/s
running	3.0 m/s
cycling	6.0 m/s
driving	14 m/s
speed of sound in air	330 m/s
airliner	250 m/s
commuter train	55 m/s
gale-force wind	16 m/s

Worked example

Describe how you can determine the average speed of a moving trolley as it moves down a slope. **(3 marks)**

When you know the distance that a body moves, and the time taken for the body to move that distance, you can use the equation, speed = distance ÷ time to determine its speed. This can be done by measuring the distance between two points that the trolley moves past and dividing it by the time taken to travel between those points, or by using light gates to measure the time for which a known length of card breaks a light beam.

Now try this

1 State what you need to measure to determine the speed of an object. **(2 marks)**

2 Explain why using light gates is better than using a stopwatch when determining the average speed of a trolley in the lab. **(2 marks)**

3 Explain why the speed of the trolley at the bottom of the slope is greater than its speed at the top of the slope. **(3 marks)**

Newton's first law

A body will remain at rest or continue in a straight line at a constant speed as long as the forces acting on it are balanced.

Stationary bodies

The forces acting on a stationary body are balanced.

The forces acting on the object are balanced — tension 25 N, weight 25 N

A common mistake is to think that when the resultant force on an object is zero, the object is stationary. The object may also be travelling at a constant speed.

Bodies moving at a constant speed

The forces acting on a body moving at a constant speed, and in a straight line, are balanced.

reaction force 15 kN, drag 20 kN, thrust 20 kN, weight 15 kN

The forces on the car are balanced. The car will continue to move at a constant speed in a straight line until another external force is applied.

Unbalanced forces

5 N   10 N

This body will accelerate to the right, since there is a resultant force of 5 N acting to the right.

Worked example

Explain the effect that each of these forces will have on a car.
(a) 300 N forward force from the engine, 200 N drag.   **(3 marks)**

Resultant force = 300 N − 200 N = 100 N. The car will accelerate in the direction of the resultant force. Its velocity will increase.

(b) 200 N forward force from the engine, 400 N friction from brakes.   **(3 marks)**

Resultant force = 200 N − 400 N = −200 N (200 N acting backwards). The car will accelerate in the direction of the resultant force. This is in the opposite direction to its velocity, so the car will slow down.

(c) 300 N forward force, 300 N drag.   **(3 marks)**

Resultant force = 0 N. The car will continue to move at the same velocity.

> A resultant force acting in the opposite direction to the movement of a body will slow it down. It can also reverse the direction of motion.

Now try this

1   State what forces act on a body that is moving at a constant speed.   **(2 marks)**

2   Explain how the direction of a moving body can be made to change.   **(2 marks)**

3   Draw diagrams to show how two forces of 100 N acting on a mass can make it:
(a) stationary   **(2 marks)**
(b) move at a constant speed   **(2 marks)**
(c) accelerate to the left.   **(2 marks)**

Newton's second law

When a resultant force acts on a mass then there will be a change in its velocity. The resultant force determines the size and direction of the subsequent acceleration of the mass.

large force in this direction

Two or more forces acting on an object can be replaced by one force. This is called the resultant force.

small force in this direction

resultant force

Forces have direction, so a force of −1 N is in the opposite direction to a force of 1 N.

When two or more forces act on the same straight line or are parallel, they can be added together to find the **resultant force**.

F_{net} is 400 N, up

F_{tens} = 1 200 N

F_{grav} = 800 N

F_{net} is 200 N, down

F_{air} = 600 N

F_{grav} = 800 N

F_{net} is 20 N, left

F_{norm} = 50 N

F_{frid} = 20 N

F_{grav} = 50 N

Force, mass and acceleration

You can calculate the acceleration of an object when you know its mass and the resultant force acting on it using the equation:

$$acceleration\ (m/s^2) = \frac{force\ (N)}{mass\ (kg)}$$

$$a = \frac{F}{m}$$

Rearrange the equation to give the force:

$$F = m \times a$$

LEARN IT!
IT'S NOT ON THE EQUATIONS LIST

* The acceleration is in the same direction as the force.
* When the resultant force is zero, the acceleration is zero.
* A negative force means that the object is accelerating backwards or is slowing down.

Worked example

The diagram shows the horizontal forces acting on a boat. The boat has a mass of 400 kg.

drag 600 N

thrust 900 N

Calculate the acceleration of the boat at the instant shown in the diagram. **(3 marks)**

resultant force on boat = 900 N – 600 N = 300 N forwards

mass = 400 kg

$$acceleration = \frac{F}{m} = \frac{300\ N}{400\ kg}$$

$$= 0.75\ m/s^2.$$

F / m × a

Make sure you include minus signs in your calculations where necessary.

Worked example

A resultant force of 6 N acts on a toy car, giving it an acceleration of 2 m/s². Calculate the mass of the toy car. **(3 marks)**

Force = mass × acceleration

Mass = force ÷ acceleration = 6 N ÷ 2 m/s²

= 3 kg

Now try this

1 Calculate the resultant force that causes a 1.2 kg mass to accelerate at 8 m/s². **(2 marks)**

2 Calculate the size of the mass that will accelerate at 2 m/s² when a resultant force of 24 N acts on it. **(3 marks)**

3 Calculate the acceleration of a car of mass 1200 kg when a resultant force of 6000 N acts on it. **(3 marks)**

Weight and mass

It is important that you understand the difference between weight and mass. These words are often used interchangeably but are actually different things.

Weight

Weight is the **force** that a body experiences due to its mass and the size of the gravitational field that it is in.

Weight is a **vector** quantity and is measured in **newtons** (N).

The weight of a body on the surface of the Earth acts inwards towards the Earth's centre.

Mass

Mass is a measure of the **amount of matter** that is contained within a three-dimensional space.

Mass is a **scalar** quantity and is measured in **kilograms** (kg).

The mass of a body is not affected by the size of the gravitational field that it is in.

Connection between mass and weight

To find the weight of an object, use the equation:

weight (N) = mass (kg) × gravitational field strength (N/kg)

$W = m \times g$

LEARN IT!
IT'S NOT ON THE EQUATIONS LIST

The weight of an object is directly proportional to the value of g, so a mass will weigh more on Earth than it does on the Moon.

Gravitational field strength

The gravitational field strength of a body, such as a planet, depends on:

① the **mass** of the body

② the **radius** of the body.

When a body has a large mass and a small radius, it will have a large gravitational field strength.

The units of gravitational field strength are newtons per kilogram (N/kg), but it can also be given as m/s^2.

Astronomical body	Value for g
Earth	10 N/kg
Moon	1.6 N/kg
Jupiter	26 N/kg
Neptune	13.3 N/kg
Mercury	3.6 N/kg
Mars	3.75 N/kg
neutron star	10^{12} N/kg

Worked example

An astronaut has a mass of 58 kg on Earth. State the astronaut's mass and weight:

(a) on the surface of the Moon   **(3 marks)**

Mass does not change so it is still 58 kg.

weight = 58 kg × 1.6 N/kg = 92.8 N

(b) on the surface of Jupiter.   **(3 marks)**

Mass does not change, so it is still 58 kg.

weight = 58 kg × 26 N/kg = 1508 N

Measuring weight

Weight is measured using a newtonmeter.

Reading the scale tells you the weight of the mass in newtons.

The greater the mass attached, the more weight it will experience due to gravity and the more the spring will stretch.

A 2 kg mass has twice the weight on Earth as a 1 kg mass, so the extension of the spring will be twice as big.

Now try this

1 Calculate the weight of a 50 kg mass when it is placed on
   (a) Earth   **(2 marks)**
   (b) Jupiter.   **(2 marks)**

2 A body has a weight of 480 N on Earth. Calculate its mass.   **(3 marks)**

3 Calculate the value for g on the surface of a planet where a mass of 18 kg experiences a weight of 54 N.   **(3 marks)**

Force and acceleration

🧪 **Practical skills** You can determine the relationship between force, mass and acceleration by varying the masses added to a trolley and measuring the time it takes to pass between two light gates that are a small distance apart.

Core practical

> There is more information about the relationship between force, mass and acceleration on pages 8 and 9.

Investigating force and acceleration

Aim

To investigate the effect of mass on the acceleration of a trolley.

Apparatus

trolley, light gates, data logger, card of known length, slope or ramp, masses

Method

1 Set up the apparatus as shown.

2 Set up the light gates to take the velocity and time readings for you.

3 Record velocity and time for different values of mass on the trolley.

4 Work out acceleration by dividing the difference in the velocity values by the time taken for the card to pass between both gates.

5 If you are changing the mass, the slope or gradient needs to remain the same throughout the investigation.

Results

The results for a slope of 20° to the horizontal and a card width of 10 cm are shown in the table below.

Mass (g)	Δv (m/s)	Δt (s)	a (m/s²)
200	7.0	2.2	3.2
400	6.7	2.1	3.2
600	6.8	2.2	3.1
800	6.9	2.1	3.3

Conclusion

The acceleration of the trolley does not depend on the mass of the trolley and will remain fairly constant throughout.

> An accelerating mass of greater than a few hundred grams can be dangerous, and may hurt somebody if it hits them at speed. Bear this in mind when designing your investigation.

> It is better to use light gates and other electronic equipment to record values as this is more accurate than using a ruler and a stopwatch.

🖩 **Maths skills** **Velocity and acceleration**

Key points to remember for this investigation are:

Acceleration is change in speed ÷ time taken, so two velocity values are needed, along with the time difference between these readings, to obtain a value for the acceleration of the trolley.

Velocity is the rate of change of displacement and acceleration is the rate of change of velocity. The word rate means 'per unit time':

$$v = \Delta x \div \Delta t \quad \text{and} \quad a = \Delta v \div \Delta t$$

Now try this

1 Explain why it is better to use light gates and a data logger than a stopwatch to record time values.   **(3 marks)**

2 Suggest how the investigation described above could be improved to obtain better results.   **(4 marks)**

3 Design a similar experiment to determine how acceleration depends on the gradient of the slope.   **(5 marks)**

Newton's third law

Newton's third law relates to bodies in equilibrium and can be applied to collisions when considering the conservation of momentum.

Action and reaction

Newton's third law states that for every action there is an equal and opposite reaction.

The action force and the reaction force **act on different bodies**.

100 N from the man

100 N from the wall

The man and wall are in equilibrium because the forces in the system are all balanced. There is no overall force in any direction.

Newton's third law examples

Watch out! Just because two forces are equal and opposite it does not always mean that they are an example of Newton's third law.

$R = -F = -mg$

$F = mg$

The reaction force of the table pushing up on the book, and the force of gravity acting downwards, are both acting on the same object – the book – so this is **not** an example of Newton's third law.

The gravitational pull of the Earth on the book and the gravitational pull of the book on the Earth **are** an example of Newton's third law, since they act on different objects, and are equal and opposite.

Worked example

Identify five action–reaction pairs that are present in the diagram. **(5 marks)**

1 The elephant's feet push backward on the ground; the ground pushes forward on its feet.

2 The right end of the right rope pulls leftward on the elephant's body; its body pulls rightward on the right end of the right rope.

3 The left end of the right rope pulls rightward on the man; the man pulls leftward on the left end of the right rope.

4 The right end of the left rope pulls leftward on the man; the man pulls rightward on the right end of the left rope.

5 The tractor pulls leftward on the left end of the left rope; the left end of the left rope pulls rightward on the tractor.

Now try this

1 State Newton's third law. **(3 marks)**

2 A goalkeeper catches a football from a penalty kick. Explain how Newton's third law applies to the goalkeeper's gloves in this situation. **(3 marks)**

Human reaction time

Human reaction time is the time between a **stimulus** occurring and a **response**. It is related to how quickly the human brain can process information and react to it.

Human reaction time

It takes a typical person between 0.20s and 0.25s to react to a stimulus. Some people, such as international cricketers, 100m sprinters and fighter pilots, train themselves to have improved reaction times.

For example, a top cricketer has a total time of 0.5s to play a batting stroke. The first 0.2s of this is the reaction time, the next 0.2s is the batsman's preparation to play the shot and the final 0.1s involves hitting the ball.

Reaction times and driving

Drivers have to react to changes in the traffic when driving. This may involve reacting to traffic lights changing colour, traffic slowing on a motorway or avoiding people or animals that may have walked in front of the vehicle.

The reaction time of humans may be affected by:

☑ tiredness ☑ distractions
☑ alcohol and drugs ☑ age.

Measuring reaction time

You can determine human reaction time by using the ruler drop test.

The reaction time is determined from the equation:

$$\text{reaction time} = \sqrt{\frac{2 \times \text{distance ruler falls}}{\text{gravitational field strength}}}$$

Repeats can be used to get a mean value for the reaction time.

A person sits with their index finger and thumb opened to a gap of about 8 cm.

A metre ruler is held, by a partner, so that it is vertical and exactly level with the person's finger and thumb, with the lowest numbers on the ruler at the bottom.

The ruler is dropped and then grasped by the other person.

Worked example

A ruler drop test is conducted five times with the same person. The results show that the five distances fallen are: 0.16m, 0.17m, 0.18m, 0.16m and 0.15m.

(a) Calculate the mean distance that the ruler drops. **(3 marks)**

mean = (0.16 + 0.17 + 0.18 + 0.16 + 0.15)
÷ 5 = 0.16 m

(b) Calculate the person's reaction time. **(3 marks)**

$$\text{reaction time} = \sqrt{\frac{2 \times 0.16}{10}} = 0.18\text{s}$$

Worked example

A driver moving at 30 km/h in her car has a reaction time of 0.25s. Calculate the distance the car travels between seeing a hazard in the road and then applying the brakes. **(4 marks)**

distance (m) = speed (m/s) × time(s)

30 km/h = 30000 m ÷ 3600 s = 8.3 m/s

distance travelled = 8.3 m/s × 0.25 s = 2.1 m

This distance for a driver is called the thinking distance. Read more about it on page 13.

Read more about it on page 13.

Now try this

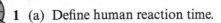

1 (a) Define human reaction time. **(1 mark)**

(b) Give three factors that can cause reaction times to increase. **(3 marks)**

2 A ruler drops a distance of 0.24m before being caught by a person. Calculate the person's reaction time. **(3 marks)**

Stopping distance

Stopping distance is the **total distance** over which a vehicle comes to rest.

It takes time for a moving car to come to a stop, and the car is still moving during this time. Understanding the factors that affect stopping distance is important for road safety.

danger appears   driver brakes   car stopped

thinking distance = the distance the car travels while the driver reacts to the danger and applies the brakes

braking distance = the distance the car travels while it is slowing down

stopping distance = thinking distance + braking distance

Factors affecting stopping distance

Thinking distance and braking distance increase when the car's speed increases.

When you double the speed of a car, the thinking distance doubles, but the braking distance increases by a factor of four.

Thinking distance (driver's reaction time) increases when:
- the driver is **tired**
- the driver is **distracted**
- the driver has taken **alcohol** or **drugs**.

Braking distance increases when:
- the amount of **friction** between the tyre and the road decreases
- the road is **icy** or **wet**
- the brakes or tyres are **worn**
- the **mass** of the car is bigger.

Thinking distance and braking distance

Thinking distance is directly proportional to speed. If the thinking distance is 6 m when the car is travelling at 20 mph, then it will be 12 m at 40 mph.

Braking distance is proportional to (speed)².

20 MPH   6 m 6 m   = 12 m (40 ft)   or 3

40 MPH   12 m   24 m   = 36 m (120 ft) or 9

To bring a vehicle to rest, work must be done on it. When a force is applied to the brakes, the kinetic energy is transferred to thermal energy and the vehicle comes to rest over a certain distance.

The equation that governs this is:

$$F \times d = \tfrac{1}{2} \times m \times v^2$$

From $F = ma$, a large deceleration exerts a large force on the people in a car. A greater force causes more serious injuries. By stopping the car over a longer time, the deceleration, and thus the force, and potential damage to the people in the car, are reduced.

Worked example

A car is moving at a constant speed. Explain how the stopping distance changes when:
(a) the speed of the car increases **(2 marks)**
(b) the car has more passengers **(2 marks)**
(c) the driver has been drinking alcohol. **(2 marks)**

(a) The stopping distance increases because the thinking distance and braking distance increase.

(b) The mass of the car will be greater so the braking distance will increase, which means the stopping distance will increase.

(c) The stopping distance will increase because the thinking distance will increase.

Now try this

1 Write down the two distances that are added to give the stopping distance of a moving vehicle. **(2 marks)**

2 Explain how the thinking and braking distance of a car changes when the speed of the car increases from 20 mph to 80 mph. **(2 marks)**

Extended response – Motion and forces

There will be one or more 6-mark questions on your exam paper. For these questions, you will need to think scientifically and structure your answer logically, showing how the points you make are related to each other. You can revise the topics for this question, which is about **motion and forces**, on pages 2–13.

Worked example

The diagram shows a trolley, ramp and light gates being used to investigate the relationship between the acceleration of a trolley on a slope and the angle that the slope makes with the horizontal.

Describe a simple investigation to determine how the acceleration of the trolley depends on the angle of the slope.

(6 marks)

I will start with the ramp at an angle of 10° and roll the trolley down the slope from the same starting position along the slope each time. The mass of the trolley needs to be kept constant, and a suitable value would be 500 g. I will then increase the ramp angle by 5° each time until I have at least 6 readings. I will repeat readings to check for accuracy and precision.

The speed of the trolley at each light gate is calculated using the equation, speed = distance ÷ time, where the distance recorded is the length of the card that passes through the light gates. The acceleration of the trolley is calculated by finding the difference in the speed values at the two light gates and then dividing this by the time it takes the trolley to pass between the gates.

I would expect the acceleration of the trolley to increase as the angle increases, although the relationship may not be linear. This is because as the slope angle increases, you increase the component of the trolley's weight that is acting down the slope, which is the force responsible for the trolley's acceleration.

Command word: Describe

When you are asked to **describe** something, you need to write down facts, events or processes accurately.

Your answer should refer to the equations needed to calculate the velocity and acceleration of the trolley, as well as how you will show the relationship between acceleration and angle of slope.

You need to be careful when stating what you will vary and what you will keep the same. Since the dependent variable is acceleration and the independent variable is angle of slope, you will need to keep the mass of the trolley and its starting point the same each time.

Be clear when referring to how the speed of the trolley will be measured by referring to the card that passes through the light gates, and mention that the length of the card needs to be known if the light gates are recording time values. You need two speed and time values to calculate the acceleration.

You can also refer to the increase in gravitational potential energy as the slope angle increases. This means more is transferred to kinetic energy and so a greater change in velocity per second.

Now try this

The distance taken for vehicles to stop on roads depends on a number of factors. Discuss what these factors are and how they affect stopping distance.

(6 marks)

Energy stores and transfers

Energy can be stored in different ways, and can be transferred from one **energy store** to another.

Examples of energy stores

There are eight main energy stores.

Energy store	Example
chemical	fuel, food, battery
kinetic	moving objects
gravitational potential	raised mass
elastic	stretched spring
thermal	hot object
magnetic	two magnets
electrostatic	two charges
nuclear	radioactive decay

Closed systems

When there are **energy transfers** in a closed system, there is no net change to the total energy in the system.

A **closed system** is one where energy can flow in or out of the system, but there is no transfer of mass. An example of a closed system is a pan of water being heated that has a lid on it so that no steam can escape.

Energy transfers

Energy is transferred from one store to another in four different ways:

- **mechanically** – by a force moving through a distance
- **electrically** – by the use of electric current
- **thermally** – because of a difference in temperature
- **radiation** – by waves such as electromagnetic or sound.

Some of the energy will be usefully transferred, and some will be wasted or **dissipated**.

Examples of energy transfers

Energy transfers from one store to another can be shown on an energy flow diagram. This one shows a battery being used to lift a mass above the ground.

Mechanical processes become wasteful when they lead to a rise in the temperature of the surroundings through heating. In all system changes, energy is stored in less useful ways. For example, the light and sound energy from a TV will eventually be absorbed by the walls and by people, leading to a rise in their temperature.

Worked example

Draw a flow diagram to show the useful and wasted energy transfers for a camping gas stove.   **(4 marks)**

In all flow diagrams, there must be energy stores and energy transfers present to show how the energy is transferred from one store to others.

Based on the law of conservation of energy, the total energy present in the original stores must be equal to the energy present in the stores after the transfers have taken place, since you cannot create or destroy energy in any given system.

Now try this

You could be asked to analyse other energy changes such as for boiling water or for moving objects.

1 Draw an energy store flow diagram for a car driving up a hill.   **(4 marks)**
2 Analyse the changes involved in the energy stores when a car accelerates with a constant force.   **(4 marks)**

Efficient heat transfer

The rate at which a material transfers thermal energy depends on a number of factors. The **efficiency** of a device is a measure of how much **useful** energy it transfers.

Thermal energy transfer

The rate at which thermal energy is transferred through a wall of a house depends on:

house wall   house wall

outside: 2°C   inside: 22°C   outside: 2°C   inside: 22°C

1 the difference in temperature between the warmer interior and the colder exterior

2 the thickness of the walls

3 the material that the walls are made from.

Efficiency

All machines **waste** some of the **energy** they **transfer**. Most machines waste energy as **heat** energy. The **efficiency** of a machine is a way of saying how good it is at transferring energy into **useful** forms.

A very efficient machine has an efficiency that is nearly 100%. The higher the efficiency, the better the machine is at transferring energy to useful forms.

Unwanted energy transfers can be reduced by thermal insulation and lubrication.

Thermal conductivity

A material with a high thermal conductivity is a better conductor of energy than one with a lower thermal conductivity. The rate at which the blue wall transfers energy is greater than that of the red wall. Different materials have different **relative thermal conductivities**.

outside: 2°C   inside: 22°C

house walls made of different materials

outside: 2°C   inside: 22°C

Worked example

A motor transfers 100 J of energy by electricity. 60 J are transferred as kinetic energy, 12 J as sound energy and 28 J as thermal energy. Calculate the efficiency of the motor.   **(3 marks)**

$$\text{efficiency} = \frac{\text{useful energy transferred by the machine}}{\text{total energy supplied to the machine}} \times 100\%$$

Efficiency does not have units.

total useful energy = 60 J

$$\text{efficiency} = \frac{60\,\text{J}}{100\,\text{J}} \times 100\%$$

$$= 60\%$$

LEARN IT!
IT'S NOT ON THE EQUATIONS LIST

No machine is ever 100% efficient. If you calculate an efficiency greater than 100% you have done something wrong!

Now try this

1 Calculate the efficiency of a lamp that transfers 14 J of energy into useful light energy for every 20 J of electrical energy input.   **(2 marks)**

2 Describe how you could reduce the rate of transfer of thermal energy through a wall.   **(2 marks)**

Energy resources

The main energy resources include both **renewable** and **non-renewable** resources.

Renewable energy resources

5 **Solar cells** convert solar energy (energy from the Sun) directly to electricity. Solar energy can also be used directly to cook food or to heat water.

1 **Bio-fuels** are animal or plant matter used to produce thermal energy, electrical energy or used to power cars.

2 **Hydroelectricity** generates electricity from water behind a dam flowing down a pipe and turning a turbine to generate electricity.

Renewable energy resources will not run out. Most do not cause pollution or emit carbon dioxide.

4 **Tidal power** uses the rise and fall of the tide or tidal currents to generate electricity.

3 **Wind turbines** use kinetic energy from the wind to generate electricity.

Non-renewable energy resources

1 **Nuclear fuels** such as uranium are used:
- to generate electricity
- as energy sources in spacecraft.

Non-renewable resources are resources that will run out eventually.

2 **Fossil fuels** are **coal**, **oil** and **natural gas**. They are used:
- to generate electricity
- to power transport
- to heat homes and for cooking.

3 Non-renewable resources are available all the time, unlike some renewable resources.

Worked example

Describe how different renewable and non-renewable resources are used for transport. **(4 marks)**

Renewable and non-renewable energy resources can both be used in power stations, leading to the production of electricity which is used to power trains. Electrical energy can also be supplied from other renewable sources such as solar, hydroelectric and wind.

Biofuel, in the form of methanol, is an example of how renewable fuel can be used to power cars, and solar power is also being developed to do more of this. Petrol and diesel, from oil, are examples of non-renewable fuels that are used to power cars.

Now try this

1　Draw diagrams to show the energy transfers that take place
　(a) in hydroelectricity　**(3 marks)**
　(b) when biofuels are used for transport.　**(3 marks)**
2　Suggest the advantages and disadvantages of using biofuels to power cars compared with using solar power to power cars.　**(4 marks)**

Patterns of energy use

The patterns and trends in how humans have used energy resources have changed over time.

Patterns and trends in energy use

The use of energy resources has changed over the years. This is because of several factors.

1. **The world's population:** in the past 200 years, the population of the world has risen from 1 billion to 7 billion people.

2. **The development of technology:** vehicles such as cars, trains and planes and other devices have increased in number and these all require energy.

3. **Electrical energy:** power stations require fuels in order to generate electricity.

Growth in world population

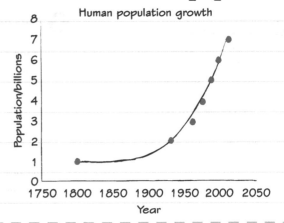

Human population growth

Trends in the world's energy use

As the graph shows, most of the world's energy use has been fossil fuels. Before about 1900, biomass in the form of wood was the major source of fuel and its use has remained constant over time.

In more recent years, there has been an increase in the use of nuclear fuel and hydroelectric power.

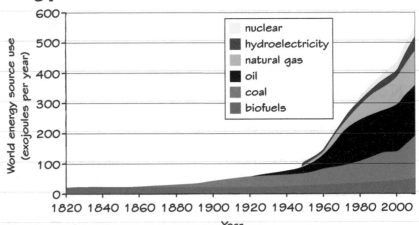

Worked example

Compare the shape of the world's population graph with that of the energy use graph. **(4 marks)**

They are similar in that as the population increases, the total energy used will increase, assuming that each person uses the same amount of energy. They differ in that the total energy use has increased faster than the population. As societies develop, they use more technology that requires energy to run it. This means that the average amount of energy used per person also increases.

The future

It is not possible to continue using the Earth's non-renewable energy reserves to the extent that they are being used now. They are a finite reserve, so will run out and not be replaced.

Greater use of fossil fuels will lead to more carbon dioxide in the atmosphere. This could cause greater global warming, leading to severe weather, flooding and threats to food supplies.

Now try this

1 Describe the main issues with using the Earth's energy supplies. **(2 marks)**

2 Wood is a biofuel. Suggest why wood has been used constantly for many years, whereas other fuels have only been used much more recently. **(3 marks)**

Potential and kinetic energy

You can calculate the **kinetic** and **gravitational potential energy** of objects using the equations on this page.

Gravitational potential energy

Gravitational potential is the energy possessed by a body due to its height above the Earth. The value of the gravitational potential energy stored depends on:

- the mass of the body
- the gravitational field strength
- the height the body is raised.

The change in gravitational potential energy is given by the equation:

$$\begin{array}{c} \text{change in gravitational} \\ \text{potential energy} \\ \text{(J)} \end{array} = \begin{array}{c} \text{mass} \\ \text{(kg)} \end{array} \times \begin{array}{c} \text{change in gravitational} \\ \text{field strength} \\ \text{(N/kg)} \end{array} \times \begin{array}{c} \text{change in} \\ \text{vertical height} \\ \text{(m)} \end{array}$$

$$\Delta GPE = m \times g \times \Delta h$$

LEARN IT! ITS NOT ON THE EQUATIONS LIST

The gravitational field strength on Earth is 10 N/kg. It can also be given in m/s².

Kinetic energy

Kinetic energy is stored in moving objects and is calculated using the equation:

$$\begin{array}{c} \text{kinetic} \\ \text{energy} \\ \text{(J)} \end{array} = \frac{1}{2} \times \begin{array}{c} \text{mass} \\ \text{(kg)} \end{array} \times \begin{array}{c} \text{(speed)}^2 \\ \text{(m/s)}^2 \end{array}$$

$$KE = \frac{1}{2} \times m \times v^2$$

LEARN IT! ITS NOT ON THE EQUATIONS LIST

Maths skills Kinetic energy is directly proportional to the mass of the moving object: doubling the mass doubles the kinetic energy of the moving object.

KE is directly proportional to the square of the speed, so doubling the speed means the KE increases by a factor of four.

Worked example

(a) A mass of 5 kg is moving at 8 m/s. Calculate its kinetic energy. **(3 marks)**

Kinetic energy = ½ × mass × velocity²

= ½ × 5 kg × (8 m/s)² = 160 J

(b) A mass of 800 g is moving at 14 m/s. Calculate its kinetic energy. **(3 marks)**

$KE = \frac{1}{2} \times m \times v^2$

$KE = \frac{1}{2} \times 0.8 \times 14^2 = 78.4$ J

Remember to square the value of speed when calculating the kinetic energy. The term v^2 means $v \times v$.

Make sure the mass is in kg and the velocity is in m/s.

Worked example

(a) A body of mass 73 kg is lifted through a vertical height of 26 m. Calculate how much gravitational potential energy it has gained. **(3 marks)**

$\Delta GPE = m \times g \times \Delta h$

= 73 kg × 10 N/kg × 26 m = 18 980 J

(b) A mass of 600 g is lifted through a vertical height of 3 m and placed on a shelf. Calculate how much gravitational potential energy the book has gained. **(3 marks)**

Change in gravitational potential energy = mass × gravitational field strength × change in height

= 0.6 kg × 10 N/kg × 3 m = 18 J

Now try this

1 A mass of 5 kg is raised through a vertical height of 18 m. Calculate the change in gravitational potential energy. **(3 marks)**

2 A girl of mass 60 kg is running with a velocity of 5 m/s. Calculate her kinetic energy. **(3 marks)**

3 A motorbike of mass 80 kg is moving at 30 km/h. Calculate its kinetic energy. **(4 marks)**

Extended response –
Conservation of energy

There will be one or more 6-mark questions on your exam paper. For these questions, you will need to think scientifically and structure your answer logically, showing how the points you make are related to each other. You can revise the topics for this question, which is about **the principle of the conservation of energy**, on pages 15–18.

Worked example

Figure 1 shows the arrangement of apparatus for a simple pendulum. Figure 2 shows how the kinetic energy of the pendulum changes with time.

Describe the energy transfers taking place during the motion of the simple pendulum. Your answer should refer to the energy stores and energy transfers that are involved.

(6 marks)

Figure 1

Figure 2

Initially, the pendulum has to be raised through a small angle, so it will gain gravitational potential energy. Once released, this gravitational potential energy store will be transferred mainly to a kinetic energy store, with some energy being dissipated as sound and heat by thermal transfer from friction due to air resistance.

The principle of conservation of energy states that the total energy of the system at any time must be the same, since energy cannot be created nor destroyed. Initially, this was all in the gravitational potential energy store, but this is then transferred to the kinetic energy store once the pendulum starts to swing. At the bottom of the swing, the gravitational potential store will be greatly reduced and the energy will be mostly in the kinetic store. Some energy is also transferred to the surroundings as heat and sound by thermal transfer from friction due to air resistance, which must also be taken into consideration as part of the total energy of the system.

Eventually, the pendulum will stop swinging, so the gravitational energy has been transferred to kinetic energy and it has eventually all ended up in the surroundings by friction due to air resistance, leading to the surroundings becoming slightly warmer. The useful energy store has been dissipated to the surroundings.

Command word: Describe

When you are asked to **describe** something, you need to write down facts, events or processes accurately.

It is a good idea to state what the principle of conservation of energy is, so that the examiner knows that you understand it. You can then apply this idea to the changes in the energy stores and transfers in the system. It is also worth noting that the way we talk about energy at GCSE now has changed – you need to refer to energy stores as well as energy transfers. In this example, the main stores are gravitational and kinetic, and the motion of the pendulum is via mechanical transfer, with energy transfer to the surroundings by thermal transfer.

In energy transfers, the energy stores are usually dissipated to the surroundings, which become warmer. In a perfect situation, with no frictional forces or energy wasted, the pendulum would swing forever, but in reality this does not happen.

Refer to *energy stores* and *energy transfers* in your answer. There are eight energy stores and four energy transfers that you need to know. See page 15 to remind yourself of these.

Now try this

The people on a small island want to use either wind power, on hills and out at sea, or its reserves of coal to generate electrical energy. Compare the advantages and disadvantages of each resource. **(6 marks)**

Waves

Waves transfer energy and information without transferring matter. Evidence of this for a water wave can be seen when a ball dropped into a pond bobs up and down, but the wave energy travels outwards as ripples across the surface of the pond.

Waves can be described by their
- **frequency** – the number of waves passing a point each second, measured in **hertz (Hz)**
- **speed** – measured in **metres per second (m/s)**
- **wavelength** and **amplitude**
- **period** – the time taken for one wavelength to pass a point
- **period** = 1/frequency.

> Watch out! Remember that the amplitude is *half* of the distance from the top to the bottom of the wave. Students often get this wrong.

Longitudinal waves

Sound waves and **seismic P waves** are **longitudinal** waves. The particles in the material the sound is travelling through move back and forth along the same direction that the sound is travelling.

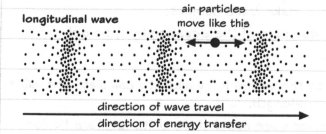

Particles in a **longitudinal** wave move **along** the same direction as the wave.

Transverse waves

Waves on a **water surface, electromagnetic waves** and **seismic S** waves are all **transverse** waves. The particles of water move in a direction at right angles to the direction the wave is travelling.

Particles in a transverse wave move **across** the direction the wave is travelling.

Give two ways in which longitudinal and transverse waves are
(a) similar **(2 marks)**

They both transfer energy without transferring matter and have an amplitude, speed, wavelength and frequency.

(b) different. **(2 marks)**

Particles in longitudinal waves vibrate along the direction of movement, whereas particles in transverse waves move at 90 degrees to the direction of travel. They can also have different speeds, frequencies and wavelengths.

Now try this

1 (a) Sketch a transverse wave and mark the amplitude and wavelength on it. **(3 marks)**
  (b) Draw an arrow to show which way the wave moves. **(1 mark)**
  (c) Draw a small particle on the wave, with arrows to show which way it moves. **(1 mark)**

2 Describe how a particle moves in a longitudinal wave. **(2 marks)**

3 The graph shows a wave. Each vertical square represents 1 mm. Work out the amplitude of the wave. **(1 mark)**

Wave equations

Both of these equations can be used to find the **speed** or **velocity** of a wave.

Speed, frequency and wavelength

$v = f \times \lambda$ v = wave speed (metres per second, m/s)

f = frequency (hertz, Hz)

λ = wavelength (metres, m)

LEARN IT!
IT'S NOT ON THE EQUATIONS LIST

Speed, distance and time

$v = \dfrac{x}{t}$ v = wave speed (metres per second, m/s)

x = distance (metres, m)

t = time (seconds, s)

LEARN IT!
IT'S NOT ON THE EQUATIONS LIST

Worked example

A seismic wave has a frequency of 15 Hz and a wavelength of 270 m. Calculate the wave speed of the seismic wave.   **(3 marks)**

Wave speed
= frequency × wavelength
= 15 Hz × 270 m
= 4050 m/s

Maths skills

To calculate wavelength, start with the equation $v = f \times \lambda$ and rearrange it to make λ the subject.

Divide both sides of the equation by f, to get

$\lambda = \dfrac{v}{f}$

Substitute the values for v and f to calculate the value for the wavelength, λ.

The units for v are m/s and the units for f are Hz (or per second), so the units for λ are $\dfrac{m/s}{1/s} = m$.

Always state the correct units as part of your answer.

Worked example

A wave on the sea travels 20 m in 5 s. Calculate the speed of the water wave.   **(3 marks)**

Speed = distance travelled ÷ time
= 20 m ÷ 5 s
= 4 m/s

Maths skills

To calculate time, rearrange the equation $v = \dfrac{x}{t}$ to give $t = \dfrac{x}{v}$.

You can also find this easily by covering the letter t in the triangle at the top of the page.

When dividing the units, m ÷ (m/s), you get m × s/m = s, which is the correct unit for time.

Again, always include the correct unit in your answer.

Now try this

1 (a) A sound wave has a wavelength of 3.3 m and a frequency of 100 Hz. Calculate its speed.   **(3 marks)**

(b) Another sound wave, with the same speed as in (a), has a frequency of 1650 Hz. Calculate its wavelength.   **(3 marks)**

2 A wave in the sea travels at 25 m/s. Calculate the distance it travels in one minute.   **(4 marks)**

Measuring wave velocity

You need to be able to **calculate** the speed of sound in air or the speed of ripples on the surface of water.

Calculating the speed of sound in air

Method 1: using an echo.

1. Measure the distance from the source of the sound to the reflecting surface (the wall).

2. Measure the time interval, with a stopwatch, between the original sound being produced and the echo being heard.

3. Use $\frac{\text{speed}}{\text{(m/s)}} = \frac{\text{distance}}{\text{(m)}} \div \frac{\text{time}}{\text{(s)}}$ to calculate the speed of sound in air.

Repeating the experiment a number of times over a range of distances will allow you to obtain accurate and precise results.

Method 2: using two microphones and an oscilloscope.

1. Set up the microphones one in front of the other at different distances in a straight line from a loudspeaker.

2. Set the frequency of the sound from the loudspeaker to a known, audible value.

3. Display the two waveforms on the oscilloscope. Measure the distance between the microphones.

4. Move the microphones apart so that the waveforms move apart by 1 wavelength.

5. Calculate the speed of sound using the equation:
$\frac{\text{wavespeed}}{\text{(m/s)}} = \frac{\text{frequency}}{\text{(Hz)}} \times \frac{\text{wavelength}}{\text{(m)}}$

Calculating the speed of ripples on water surfaces

You can work out the speed of ripples on the surface of water using a ripple tank and a strobe.

Set the power supply to vibrate the paddle at a known frequency.

lamp

water

plane waves

image of waves on screen

Use a strobe light to 'freeze' the water waves so that you can measure the wavelength.

strobe light

Use the equation *wave speed = frequency × wavelength* to calculate the speed or velocity of the water waves on the surface of the ripple tank.

Worked example

(a) A hand clap is made 480 m from a wall and the echo is heard 3 seconds later. Calculate the speed of sound. **(3 marks)**

speed = distance ÷ time = 960 m ÷ 3 s = 320 m/s

(b) Method 2 is used to determine the speed of sound. The distance between the two microphones is 35 cm and it represents one wavelength. The frequency of the sound is 1 kHz. Calculate the speed of sound in air. **(3 marks)**

wave speed = frequency × wavelength = 1000 Hz × 0.35 m = 350 m/s

Now try this

1. A wave on the sea travels 30 m in 5 s. Calculate the speed of the wave. **(3 marks)**
2. The frequency of a ripple tank paddle is 4 Hz and the wavelength of the ripples is 8 cm. Calculate the speed of the water waves in m/s. **(3 marks)**
3. Describe how you could obtain an accurate value for the speed of sound in air. **(4 marks)**

Waves and boundaries

Waves can show different effects when they move from one material to another. These changes can occur at the **boundary** or **interface** between the two materials.

Waves and boundaries

Whenever a sound wave, light wave or water wave reaches the boundary between two materials, the wave can be:

- **reflected**
- **refracted**
- **transmitted** or
- **absorbed**.

Different substances reflect, refract, transmit or absorb waves in ways that vary with the wavelength.

Different wavelengths of radiation are absorbed by molecules in the atmosphere by different amounts.

Changes in sound waves

When sound waves move from one material into another material, there can be a change in their velocity.

- If sound waves move from a less dense to a more dense material, the sound waves will speed up.
- The frequency of the sound waves does not change.
- If the velocity changes, then the wavelength must increase, since

wave speed = frequency × wavelength.

Refraction

Sound waves, water waves and light waves can all be refracted. Refraction can result in a change of direction. The direction does not change if the wavefronts travel perpendicular to the normal.

Sound waves travel faster in warmer air than in cooler air, as the molecules move faster in warmer air.

Water waves change direction and bend towards the normal when they move from deep water to shallow water.

Light waves bend towards the normal when they move from air into glass. They bend away from the normal when they move from glass back into air.

Worked example

Sound waves travel from water into the air. Describe what happens to the sound waves when they are travelling perpendicular to the boundary between water and air. **(3 marks)**

The frequency of the sound wave remains the same but its wavelength and velocity change. The direction of the wave does not change.

Refraction special case

When light, sound or water waves move from one material into another their **direction does not change** if they are moving along the normal.

Now try this

1 State four things that can happen to a sound wave at a boundary between two materials. **(2 marks)**
2 Describe the changes that can happen to a sound wave when it moves from warm air into cold air.
   (3 marks)

Waves in fluids

 Practical skills You can **determine the wave speed, frequency and wavelength** of waves by using appropriate apparatus.

See pages 21–23 for the properties of waves, including the relationship between wave speed, frequency and wavelength.

Core practical

Investigating waves

Aim

To investigate the suitability of apparatus to measure the speed, frequency and wavelength of waves in a fluid.

Apparatus

ripple tank, motor, plane wave generator, stroboscope, ruler, A3 paper and pencil

Water and electricity are being used here, both of which can be dangerous. Be careful to take this into consideration when planning your practical.

Method

1 Set up the apparatus as shown below.

2 Calculate the frequency of the waves by counting the number of waves that pass a point each second. Do this for a minute and then divide by 60 to get a more accurate value for the frequency of the water waves.

To obtain accurate results for the wavelength of the water wave, it is best to find the distance between a large number of waves and then divide this value by the number of waves. This will reduce the percentage error in your value when determining a value for the wavelength of the wave.

3 Use a stroboscope to 'freeze' the waves and find their wavelength by using a ruler. The ruler can be left in the tank or the waves can be projected onto a piece of A3 paper under the tank and the wave positions marked with pencil marks on the paper.

4 Calculate the wave speed.

Results

Wavelength (m)	Frequency (Hz)	Wave speed (m/s)
0.05	10.0	5.0
0.10	5.0	5.0
0.15	3.0	4.5
0.20	2.5	5.0

Waves in water

Water waves will travel at a constant speed in a ripple tank when generated at different frequencies if the depth of the water is constant at all points. This means that the equation wave speed = frequency × wavelength will give the same wave speed – if the frequency increases, then the wavelength will decrease in proportion.

Conclusion

A ripple tank can be used to determine values for the wavelength, frequency and wave speed of water waves. It is a suitable method, provided that small wavelengths and frequencies are used.

Now try this

1 State the two equations that can be used to calculate wave speed. **(2 marks)**

2 When a water wave moves from shallow water to deep water its wavelength increases. Explain why the wave velocity will also increase.

(3 marks)

Extended response – Waves

There will be one or more 6-mark questions on your exam paper. For these questions, you will need to think scientifically and structure your answer logically, showing how the points you make are related to each other. You can revise the topics for this question, which is about **waves**, on pages 21–25.

Worked example

Waves transfer energy without there being any overall transfer of matter.

These waves can be modelled using a slinky spring, as shown in Figure 1 and Figure 2.

Explain how the wave motion that occurs is related to the disturbance that is causing it and the material that it is moving in.

Your answer should refer to real-life examples of both types of waves. **(6 marks)**

Figure 1

Figure 2

wavelength

Figure 1 shows a longitudinal wave. A longitudinal wave is produced when the vibration is parallel to the direction of energy transfer.

Figure 2 shows a transverse wave. A transverse wave is produced when the vibration or oscillation is at right angles to the direction of energy transfer.

Sound waves, infrasound and ultrasound waves are all examples of longitudinal waves, as are seismic P waves. These waves can only transfer energy if there is a medium (a solid, liquid or gas) for them to travel through. Some transverse waves also travel through matter, with examples including water waves and seismic S waves.

Unlike longitudinal waves, some transverse waves can travel through a vacuum and do not need a medium. This is the case for all electromagnetic waves.

The wave in Figure 1 has correctly been identified as a longitudinal wave. A simple description of how it is produced is also given.

The wave in Figure 2 has correctly been identified as a transverse wave. There is also a simple description of how it is produced.

Command word: Explain

When you are asked to **explain** something, it is not enough to just state or describe something. Your answer **must** contain some reasoning or justification of the points you make.

After identifying the waves correctly, examples are given of these waves and the fact that longitudinal waves require a medium. Transverse waves can also do this, but one distinct difference is that transverse electromagnetic waves can travel through space.

All electromagnetic waves are transverse and all sound waves are longitudinal in nature. In terms of seismic waves, think of the letter 's' – a **s**eismic **S**-wave is tran**s**verse. These **S** waves will only travel through **s**olids. Unlike P waves, they will **not** travel through liquids such as the Earth's liquid outer core.

Now try this

Describe an experiment to show that with water and sound waves it is the wave, and not the water or air, itself that travels.
(6 marks)

Reflection and refraction

Reflection and **refraction** are two properties of all types of waves.

Reflection

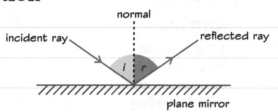

The **normal** is a line drawn at 90° to the mirror surface at the point that the arriving or incident ray meets the mirror. The angles *i* and *r* are measured from this line.

The law of reflection is　angle *i* = angle *r*

When sketching ray diagrams you do not need to get the angles exactly right, but the sketch should not appear to ignore the rule. If you are asked to *plot* a ray diagram, use a protractor to measure the angles.

Refraction

Refraction is the change in the direction of a light ray that happens when it travels from one transparent material into another. Notice that the ray of light bends *towards* the normal as it enters the glass and *away* from the normal when it leaves the glass.

Rays of light that meet a surface at 90° do not bend at all but simply continue into the material without a change in direction.

Worked example

(a) Explain what happens during refraction.
(3 marks)

The velocity of the wave changes as it moves from one medium to another. Its direction also changes unless it is travelling along the normal.

(b) Explain what happens when light enters glass from air.
(3 marks)

The direction of the wave changes unless it is travelling along the normal. The light wave will bend towards the normal. This is called refraction.

Worked example

(a) State the law of reflection.　**(1 mark)**

The angle of incidence is equal to the angle of reflection.

(b) A light ray hits the surface of a mirror at 28° to the normal. At what angle will it be reflected?　**(3 marks)**

It will be reflected at 28° to the normal.

Now try this

1 A ray of light strikes a plane mirror at 42° to the normal. State the angle of reflection.
(1 mark)

2 A ray of light is travelling through a glass block before entering into air. The angle of incidence in the glass block is 34°. Estimate the angle of refraction once it has entered the air and give a reason.　**(2 marks)**

3 Describe what happens when a light ray moves from glass into air.　**(3 marks)**

Total internal reflection

Total internal reflection involves both **reflection** and **refraction**.

The role of refraction

Refraction is when light slows down and usually changes direction when it travels from a less dense to a more dense medium.

Light slows down and bends towards the normal when moving from air into glass or water.

The role of reflection

As the angle of incidence increases, the angle of refraction will increase until it reaches 90°. At this point, the ray of light is travelling along the outer surface of the glass. The angle of incidence is the **critical angle**.

Above the **critical angle**, the light is totally internally reflected.

Critical angles

Total internal reflection can only occur when light travelling from a **dense** material like glass meets a boundary with a **less dense** material like air.

Light speeds up and changes direction away from the normal when it travels from glass into air.

Total internal reflection can take place with sound as well as light.

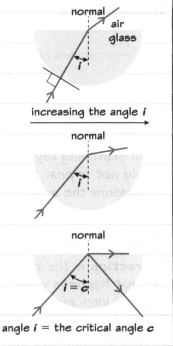

increasing the angle *i*

angle *i* = the critical angle *c*

total internal reflection
angle *i* > critical angle *c*

Worked example

(a) Draw a labelled diagram to show how total internal reflection (TIR) is used in optical fibres.   **(3 marks)**

Rays of light meeting the boundary between the cladding and the core are totally internally reflected.

(b) Explain the two conditions necessary for total internal reflection to take place.   **(2 marks)**

1. The cladding must have a smaller refractive index (lower density) than the core.
2. The waves must meet the boundary at an angle greater than the critical angle.

Endoscopes

Endoscopes can be used to look inside patients' bodies, and make use of optical fibres. Endoscopes allow 'keyhole' surgery. This is surgery conducted through a very small cut in the body to speed up recovery time.

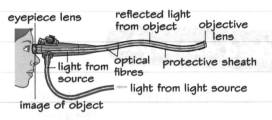

Now try this

1 State what is meant by the term critical angle.   **(2 marks)**
2 The critical angle for two materials that are in contact is 45°. Explain what will happen to the incident ray if it has an angle of incidence of 60°.   **(3 marks)**
3 Describe the conditions for total internal reflection to occur for a ray of light.   **(3 marks)**

Colour of an object

The colour an object appears is related to the **transmission**, **reflection** and **absorption** of different wavelengths of light.

Specular reflection

Specular reflection occurs when waves are reflected from a smooth surface.

When parallel rays of light are incident on a **smooth**, plane surface such as a mirror, the reflected light rays will also be **parallel**.

The sizes of any irregularities on the surface are much smaller than the wavelength of the wave.

Diffuse reflection

Diffuse reflection occurs when the surface is **not smooth** and has rough irregularities. The size of the irregularities is comparable with the wavelength of the wave. The incident wave is then reflected at **many different angles** and the reflected rays will not be parallel, such as when light is reflected off a painted wall.

The colour spectrum

Visible light makes up a very small part of the electromagnetic spectrum. The colours that we see can be split into different colours by a prism.

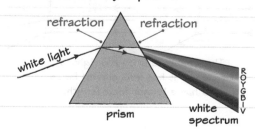

These colours all have a different wavelength, ranging from the longest wavelength at the red end of the spectrum to the shortest wavelength at the violet end.

Differential absorption at surfaces

The colour an object appears is based on how the atoms at its surface respond to the light being shone on them. A material appears green because its atoms reflect the green wavelengths and absorb all of the others.

Filters

Filters let through different colours of light and absorb all other colours. For example, a green filter will let through or 'transmit' green light and absorb all of the other wavelengths.

Worked example

Explain which type of reflection you would associate with a plane mirror or a calm lake surface. **(2 marks)**

specular reflection, because the surface is smooth, so parallel rays or wavefronts that are incident on these surfaces will be reflected as parallel rays or wavefronts

Now try this

1 Explain which type of reflection you would associate with a gravel path. **(2 marks)**

2 Explain how a filter works to let through red light. **(2 marks)**

3 Explain why a blue surface looks blue when white light is shone onto it. **(3 marks)**

Lenses and power

Lenses are pieces of **glass** that **bend light** in order to bring it to a **focus**. Lenses make use of **refraction** to bend light. The more refraction that occurs, the more **power** the lens has.

Lenses and refraction

Lenses use refraction to bend light. There are two main types of lens – a **converging** lens and a **diverging** lens.

Lenses that are thicker in the middle are **converging** lenses and those that are thinner in the middle are **diverging** lenses.

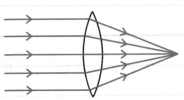

converging lens

A converging lens bends rays of light towards one another, bringing them to a point.

diverging lens

A diverging lens bends rays of light away from each other.

Power of a lens

The greater the **power** of a lens, the more it bends light. This is related to the **shape** of the lens.

Parallel rays of light all converge to pass through f.

 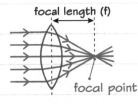

focal length (f)   focal length (f)

focal point   focal point

The stronger lens on the right is fatter so it has more sharply curved faces and has a shorter focal length.

Parallel rays of light diverge so that they all seem to come from f.

 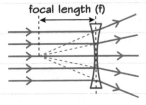

focal length (f)   focal length (f)

The weaker lens on the right is thinner so it has less curved faces and has a longer focal length.

Worked example

Describe how the following lenses compare in terms of their (a) powers and (b) focal lengths.   **(2 marks)**

lens X   lens Y

(a) Lens X is more powerful than lens Y.

(b) Lens Y has a longer focal length than lens X.

For lenses made of the same type of glass, the thicker, more curved lens will have the greater power and shorter focal length.

Now try this

1 Explain how the power of a lens is related to its shape.   **(2 marks)**

2 What is the relationship between the power of a lens and its focal length?   **(1 mark)**

3 Suggest another factor, apart from thickness, that would change the power of a lens.   **(1 mark)**

Real and virtual images

The images produced by a lens depend on the **type of lens** being used and the **position of the object** with respect to the lens.

Real images and converging lenses

When parallel light rays from a distant object pass through a converging lens, they are brought to a focus at a point – the **focal point** or **principal focus**. The object can be said to be 'at infinity' if its distance from the lens is much greater than the focal length of the lens.

A **real image** is an image that can be **produced on a screen**. The lens focuses light rays at the screen.

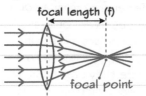

focal length (f)

focal point

> The focal length depends on the **thickness** of the lens and the **material** that the lens is made from.

> A **real image** is formed where light rays **converge** and are **actually focused** on a screen.

The nature of a real image

Far from the lens, the real image is upside down and smaller than the object.

$2F_1$ F_1 O F_2 $2F_2$

Moving the object closer to the lens causes the image to become larger. The position of the image will move away from the lens but will remain real and upside down.

object   object

2F F   F 2F   2F F   F 2F
        image   image

At a distance of twice the focal length (2F), the object and image are the same size. Between F and 2F, the image is magnified.

Virtual images, converging and diverging lenses

A **virtual image** is formed by a converging lens when the object is between the focal point and the lens.

image converging lens

F
F object

magnifying glass

A diverging lens produces a virtual image.

object outside focal point   object inside focal point

> A **virtual image** is formed by light rays which **appear** to **diverge** from that point, but do not actually do so.

Worked example

State what type of image is formed by:
(a) the human eye   **(1 mark)**

a real image

(b) a magnifying glass.   **(1 mark)**

a virtual image

Now try this

1 State what type of image is produced on a screen at the cinema.   **(1 mark)**

2 Draw a ray diagram to show what happens to rays of light when an object is placed at a distance of 3F from the lens.   **(3 marks)**

Electromagnetic spectrum

Infrared radiation, **visible light** and **ultraviolet radiation** are all part of the **electromagnetic spectrum**.

All electromagnetic waves...

- are **transverse waves** (the electromagnetic vibrations are at right angles to the direction the wave is travelling – see page 21)
- travel at the **same speed** (3×10^8 m/s) in a **vacuum**
- **transfer energy** to the observer.

Watch out!

The different parts of the electromagnetic spectrum have different properties, which you will read about on the following pages. But it is important to remember that some of their properties are *the same*. They are *all* transverse waves, and *all* travel at the same speed in a vacuum.

The electromagnetic spectrum

As the **frequency** of the radiation **increases**, the **wavelength decreases**.

longest wavelength
lowest frequency

shortest wavelength
highest frequency

10^3 m   1 m 10^{-3} m 10^{-6} m 10^{-9} m 10^{-12} m

← radio waves → ← micro- → ← infrared → ← X-rays →
waves

ultra-violet
rays (UV)

gamma
← rays →

Wavelengths within the spectrum are put into groups.

visible spectrum

All electromagnetic waves transfer energy from a source to the observer. For example, radio waves are sent from a transmitting antenna to a TV where they are 'seen' as TV images; microwaves are sent from mobile phones and received by another person; and infrared radiation can be 'seen' by infrared cameras when given off by hot bodies.

Worked example

(a) List the main groups of electromagnetic waves from longest to shortest wavelength.   **(1 mark)**

radio, microwave, infrared, visible, ultraviolet, X-rays, gamma

(b) A wave has a wavelength of 100 m and a frequency of 3 000 000 Hz. Calculate its wave speed.   **(3 marks)**

Wave speed = frequency × wavelength =
300 000 000 Hz × 100 m
= 300 000 000 m/s

(c) Explain why this wave must be an electromagnetic wave.   **(1 mark)**

Electromagnetic waves all travel at 300 000 000 m/s in air.

You can use a mnemonic to help you to remember the order. A mnemonic is a sentence or phrase whose words have the same initial letters as the list you are trying to remember. For example:
Red Monkeys In Vans Use X-ray Glasses.

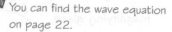

You can find the wave equation on page 22.

Now try this

1. State the type of electromagnetic radiation that has the (a) longest wavelength, (b) highest frequency.   **(2 marks)**

2. Calculate the speed of a radio wave in air if it has a wavelength of 3000 m and a frequency of 100 000 Hz.   **(2 marks)**

3. Calculate the frequency of a microwave that has a wavelength of 5 cm in air. Take the speed of light in air to be 300 000 000 m/s.   **(4 marks)**

Investigating refraction

 Practical skills You can investigate refraction in rectangular glass blocks in terms of the interaction of light waves with matter.

Core practical

Aim

To investigate the nature of how light waves change direction when they move from air into glass.

Apparatus

ray box and slits, 12 V power supply, glass block, protractor, A3 paper, sharp pencil

Method

1. Place the rectangular block on the A3 paper and draw around it with the sharp pencil.

2. Draw the normal line, which will be at right angles to the side of the block towards which the light ray will be shone.

3. Using the protractor and pencil, mark on the paper angles of incidence of 0° through to 80° in 10° intervals.

4. Starting with the 0° angle (the light ray travelling along the normal line), direct the light ray towards the block and mark its exit point from the block with a sharp pencil dot.

5. Remove the glass block and join the dot to the point of incidence by drawing a straight line. Measure and record this angle, which is the angle of refraction.

6. Repeat for all of the other angles from 10° to 80°.

glass box

normal

ray box

Results

Angle of incidence	Angle of refraction
0°	0°
10°	7°
20°	13°
30°	19°
40°	25°
50°	31°
60°	35°

Conclusion

When a light ray travels from air into a glass block, its direction changes and the angle of refraction will be less than the angle of incidence unless it is travelling along the normal.

There is more information about the refraction of light on pages 27 and 28.

When carrying out the investigation, make sure that you direct a thin beam of light towards the point at which the normal makes contact with the glass block. Clearly mark the angles from 0° to 80° with a sharp pencil and ruler.

Refraction

The refraction of a light ray involves a change in:

- ✓ the direction of the light ray
- ✓ the speed of the light.

Light slows down when it moves from air into glass and speeds up when it moves from glass into air.

The only time when the direction does not change is when the beam is travelling along the normal.

Remember that the angle of incidence is measured with respect to the normal line.

Light will slow down more when it travels from air into glass than it will when it travels from air into water. This is because the 'optical density' of glass is greater than that of air.

Now try this

1. State the two things that can change when a light ray is refracted. **(2 marks)**

2. Draw a table of results for a light ray travelling from air into a block of water instead of a block of glass. **(2 marks)**

3. Explain how the (a) frequency and (b) wavelength of a light ray are affected when it enters glass from air. **(4 marks)**

EM radiation and temperature

All objects above absolute zero will **emit** electromagnetic radiation. The **intensity** and the **wavelength** of the radiation depend on the temperature of the body.

Emitting radiation

A hot cup of tea at 90°C will emit radiation that is mainly in the **infrared part** of the EM spectrum, whereas the Sun's surface temperature of 5700°C means that it emits **visible light** and **ultraviolet** radiation which have a shorter wavelength than infrared. Bodies that are much hotter than the Sun will emit **X-rays**.

Wave velocities

Electromagnetic waves have different velocities in different materials. This is linked, to an extent, to the density of the material. The speed of light in a diamond is around 40% of the speed of light in a vacuum or air, due to the high optical density of diamond.

Intensity and wavelength

Intensity is the energy emitted per square metre per second – or the power emitted per square metre. The intensity and wavelength of the radiation emitted by a body depend on its temperature.

As the surface temperature of the body increases:

1 the intensity of the radiation it emits increases

2 the wavelength that corresponds to the peak intensity decreases.

The graph shows the relationship between surface temperature, intensity and peak wavelength.

Worked example

(a) Compare the intensity of radiation emitted from a cup of tea at 80°C with a bonfire at 1000°C. **(2 marks)**

The bonfire is at a much higher temperature, so the intensity of the emitted radiation will be much greater compared to the cup of tea.

(b) Compare the peak wavelength of the radiation emitted by the tea with that of the bonfire. **(2 marks)**

The peak wavelength is lower for the bonfire than it is for the tea. This is because the peak wavelength decreases as the temperature increases.

Hot objects such as a hot cup of tea will emit infrared radiation. You can feel this radiation on your skin as thermal energy but you cannot detect it with your eyes. As objects get hotter, they start to emit shorter wavelengths which are part of the visible spectrum. This is why you can see the bonfire as well as feel the infrared from it – the peak wavelengths are detected by the eye.

Now try this

1 State the factor that affects the intensity and wavelength of the radiation emitted by a body. **(1 mark)**

2 Compare the intensity of the radiation emitted from a block of ice at 0°C with a pan of water at 90°C. **(2 marks)**

3 Explain why some stars appear red whereas others appear blue. **(4 marks)**

Thermal energy and surfaces

Practical skills You can investigate the relationship between the **rate** at which a material **emits** or **absorbs thermal radiation** and the nature of its **surface**.

Core practical

> There is more information on the emission and absorption of thermal energy on page 34.

Aim

To investigate how the nature of a surface affects the rate at which it absorbs or radiates thermal energy.

Apparatus

Leslie's cube, thermometers, stopwatch, ruler, clamp, boss and retort stand.

Method 1: radiating thermal energy

1 Fill Leslie's cube with hot water at a known temperature. Place a thermometer a small distance away from each of the sides. Plug the top of the cube with a bung.

2 Measure the temperature at a distance of 10 cm from each of the four sides of Leslie's cube for a period of 5 minutes, taking a reading every 30 seconds.

> Be careful when using hot water as it may scald.

> Conduct the investigation accurately and fairly by ensuring that the thermometer used is the same for each surface, the distance from the surface is the same and the starting temperature is the same in each case. Take the same number of readings over the same time period and intervals.

Method 2: absorbing thermal energy

1 Fill Leslie's cube with the same volume of cold water at a known temperature. Plug the top of the cube with a thermometer and bung.

2 Heat each side, one at a time, with a radiant heater from the same distance away (about 10 cm).

3 Record how the temperature of the water changes, every 30 seconds, over an appropriate period of time.

Results

Method 1: Plot graphs of temperature against time for each of the four surfaces on the same axes.

	Dull black	Shiny black	Shiny white	Dull white
Start	80 °C	80 °C	80 °C	80 °C
Finish	56 °C	62 °C	74 °C	68 °C

Method 2: Plot a graph of temperature against time.

	Dull black	Shiny black	Shiny white	Dull white
Start	20 °C	20 °C	20 °C	20 °C
Finish	34 °C	28 °C	22 °C	24 °C

Conclusion

Typical results obtained are shown in the table.

	Dull black	Shiny black	Silver	Dull white
Emitter	Best	2nd	3rd	Worst
Absorber	Best	2nd	3rd	Worst

Leslie's cube

Leslie's cube is commonly used in schools to demonstrate how the nature of a surface affects the rate at which thermal energy is absorbed or emitted.

Four of its sides have different natures, as shown.

 Now try this

1 Sketch four curves on a temperature–time graph for the four sides of a Leslie's cube that has been filled with hot water. **(4 marks)**

2 Explain why the starting temperature for the Leslie's cube practical needs to be kept constant. **(4 marks)**

Dangers and uses

The amount of **energy** that is transferred by an electromagnetic wave is dependent on its **wavelength** or **frequency**. The **highest frequencies** (shortest wavelengths) are the most energetic and the **most dangerous** waves.

Dangers

high frequency

Uses

X-rays and gamma-rays can cause mutations (changes) to the DNA in cells in the body. This may kill the cells or cause **cancer**.

gamma-rays

- to sterilise food and medical equipment
- in scanners to detect cancer
- to treat cancer

X-rays

- to look inside objects, including medical x-rays to look inside bodies
- in airport security scanners, to see what people have in their luggage

UV in sunlight can damage skin cells, causing **sunburn**. Over time, exposure to UV can cause **skin cancer**. UV can also damage the **eyes** leading to eye conditions.

ultraviolet

- to detect security marks made using special pens
- inside fluorescent lamps
- to detect forged banknotes (real banknotes have markings that glow in UV light)
- to disinfect water

visible light

- allows us to see, lights up rooms and streets, buildings and roads (illumination)
- photography

Infrared radiation transfers thermal energy. Too much infrared radiation can cause **skin** burns.

infrared

- in cooking (by grills and toasters)
- to make thermal images (images using heat), used by police and rescue services
- in short-range communications, such as between laptops or other small computers
- in remote controls for TVs and other appliances, where the signal only has to travel short distances
- to send information along optical fibres
- in security systems such as burglar alarms, to detect people moving around

Microwaves heat water – so they can heat the water inside our bodies. Heating cells can damage or kill them.

microwaves

- in mobile phones, and to communicate by satellite transmissions
- for cooking (in microwave ovens)

radio waves

low frequency

- broadcasting radio and TV programmes
- communicating with ships, aeroplanes and satellites

Worked example

State which type(s) of electromagnetic radiation are:

(a) used for communicating **(4 marks)**

radio waves, microwaves, infrared and visible light

(b) used for cooking **(2 marks)**

microwave and infrared

(c) used for cleaning things **(2 marks)**

ultraviolet and gamma

(d) most dangerous. **(3 marks)**

ultraviolet, X-rays and gamma

Radio waves can be produced by, or can themselves induce, oscillations in electrical circuits.

The different types of electromagnetic radiation share uses and dangers. For example, more than one type can be used for communicating and cooking, and there are three main types of electromagnetic radiation that can cause humans serious harm.

Now try this

1 State the dangers associated with ultraviolet radiation. **(3 marks)**

2 Explain how X-rays are useful to doctors but can also be harmful to patients. **(3 marks)**

3 Explain how gamma-rays can be used to detect cancer even though they can also cause it. **(2 marks)**

Changes and radiation

Radiation is **absorbed** or **emitted** when **electrons** jump between **energy levels**.

Energy levels

Electrons can only exist in atoms at certain, well-defined energy levels. These **energy levels** depend on the atom, and the electrons inside the atom can move between the shells or leave the atom completely.

Electromagnetic radiation is **emitted** or **absorbed** by atoms based on whether energy is given out or taken in.

Electrons move up energy levels when they absorb energy and they fall down to lower energy levels when they emit energy.

Electrons move from a lower energy level to a higher energy level when the correct amount of energy is absorbed.

Electromagnetic radiation is emitted when electrons fall down from a higher to a lower energy level.

The electromagnetic radiation can have a **wide frequency range**, from **infrared** through to **ultraviolet** and beyond.

Atom absorbs energy.
Atom emits energy.

Nuclear radiation

Energy is also emitted from the **nuclei** of **unstable** atoms. **Protons** and **neutrons** also occupy **energy levels** in the nucleus, in the same way that electrons do in the atom.

When energy changes occur in the nucleus, high-energy **gamma-rays** are emitted.

Gamma-rays can be emitted over a large range of frequencies, depending on the energy levels within the nucleus.

protons
gamma rays
neutrons

 Worked example

Explain the energy changes that occur within the electron levels of the atom. **(3 marks)**

Electrons can move between energy levels if they absorb or emit electromagnetic radiation. When they absorb electromagnetic radiation they move up energy levels and when they emit electromagnetic radiation they move down energy levels.

The energy of electromagnetic radiation that is emitted or absorbed has to **match** the difference between the **energy levels** that the **electron** is moving between.

Energy changes in the **nucleus** are far greater than those seen between electron energy levels.

  Now try this

1 Name the two places in the atom where energy levels are found. **(2 marks)**

2 Describe what happens when electrons
   (a) absorb electromagnetic radiation **(2 marks)**
   (b) emit electromagnetic radiation. **(2 marks)**

Extended response – Light and the electromagnetic spectrum

There will be one or more 6-mark questions on your exam paper. For these questions, you will need to think scientifically and structure your answer logically, showing how the points you make are related to each other. You can revise the topics for this question, which is about **light and the electromagnetic spectrum**, on pages 27–37.

Worked example

Exposure to certain types of electromagnetic radiation can have harmful effects on the human body.

Describe how exposure to electromagnetic radiation can be harmful.

Your answer should refer to the types of electromagnetic radiation and the damage that they may cause.   **(6 marks)**

long wavelength,   short wavelength,
low frequency   high frequency

radio waves · microwaves · infrared · visible light · ultraviolet · X-rays · gamma-rays

Apart from radio waves and visible light, which are not deemed to cause damage to humans, the other five members of the electromagnetic spectrum do cause harmful effects.

Microwaves are absorbed by water molecules and can lead to internal heating of body cells, which can be harmful. Infrared radiation can cause burns to the skin.

Ultraviolet radiation can damage the eyes, leading to eye conditions. It can also cause skin cancer as surface cells are affected. X-rays and gamma-rays can both lead to cellular damage and mutations, which can lead to diseases such as cancer.

The initial sentence states which types of electromagnetic wave are dangerous and which are not. This will help to structure the rest of the answer.

Two of the low-energy members of the electromagnetic spectrum are commented on next.

The three higher-energy electromagnetic waves are then commented on. The energy of electromagnetic radiation is related directly to its frequency, so as frequency increases, so does the energy and so does the extent of the damage.

UV, X-rays and gamma-rays are examples of **ionising radiation**. This can lead to tissue damage and possible mutations in cells. Although not mentioned here, you could be asked a question that relates specifically to the dangers of ionising radiation. Of the three types mentioned here, only gamma rays come from the nucleus of the atom. You can read more about this on pages 39–56.

Command word: Describe

When you are asked to **describe** something, you need to write down facts, events or processes accurately.

Now try this

Describe how the electromagnetic spectrum is useful to humans. Refer to specific members of the EM spectrum in your answer.   **(6 marks)**

Structure of the atom

There is a very big difference in the sizes of **atoms, nuclei** and **molecules.**

Structure of the atom

Atoms have a **nucleus** containing **protons** and **neutrons. Electrons** move around the nucleus of an atom. An atom has the same number of protons and electrons, so the **+** and **–** **charges** balance and the atom has no overall charge.

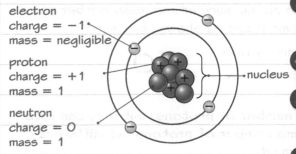

electron
charge = −1
mass = negligible

proton
charge = +1
mass = 1

neutron
charge = 0
mass = 1

nucleus

The atom and the nucleus

1 All atoms have a **nucleus.** The **nucleus** is always **positively charged** as it contains **protons** which have a positive charge and neutrons which do not have a charge.

2 The **nucleus** contains more than **99%** of the **mass** of the atom.

3 The total number of **protons** in an atom's **nucleus** must be the same as the total number of **electrons** in the shells.

4 Electrons in atoms always orbit the **nucleus** and have a **negative charge.**

5 Atoms are always **neutral** because the positive charge from the **protons** cancels out the negative charge from the **electrons.**

6 The **nucleus** of an atom of an element may contain **different numbers of neutrons.**

Atom, nucleus and molecule

A **molecule** is two or more atoms bonded together. A **molecule** is about 10 times the diameter of an atom and about 10^6 times the diameter of a nucleus.

10^{-9} m 10^{-10} m $10^{-15} - 10^{-14}$ m

molecule   atom   nucleus

Gases such as oxygen and carbon dioxide are **molecules.** Water is also a **molecule.**

The diameter of an atom is about 10^{-10} m. The diameter of the nucleus is about 10^{-15} m.

Diagrams of atoms are always incorrect in terms of the scale. In reality, if the nucleus were the size shown here, the nearest electron would be at least 1000 m away.

Worked example

A molecule has a length of 4.8×10^{-9} m. A nucleus has a diameter of 1.2×10^{-15} m. How many nuclei would need to be placed side by side in a line to have the same length as the molecule? **(3 marks)**

4.8×10^{-9} m $\div 1.2 \times 10^{-15}$ m

$\qquad = 4 \times 10^6$ or 4 million nuclei.

> 🖩 **Maths skills** Beware! A number written as 19.3 $\times 10^3$ is not written in standard form. The first number needs to be between 1 and 10, so the proper way to write this would be 1.93×10^4. Notice how the power has increased from 3 to 4 as the number at the front has become 10 times smaller.

> Remember, $-9 - (-15)$ is equal to 6 because two minuses make a plus, so $-9 + 15 = 6$.

Now try this

How many times bigger than the diameter of the nucleus is:

(a) the diameter of the atom   **(2 marks)**
(b) the diameter of a molecule?   **(2 marks)**

Atoms and isotopes

Atoms of the same **element** can be **different** based on the composition of their **nuclei**.

Atoms

Atoms are made up of **protons**, **neutrons** and **electrons**. The **protons** and **neutrons** are in the nucleus of the atom, and the **electrons** move around the outside.

proton neutron electron

not to scale

Describing atoms

All the atoms of a particular element have the same number of **protons**. The number of protons in each atom of an element is called the **atomic number**, or **proton number**.

The total number of protons and neutrons in an atom is the **mass number**, or **nucleon number**.

The atomic number and mass number of an element can be shown like this:

mass number ⟶ $^{16}_{8}O$ ⟵ atomic number

Isotopes

Atoms of a particular element always have the **same number of protons**, but they can have **different numbers of neutrons**. Atoms with the **same number of protons** but **different numbers of neutrons** are **isotopes** of the same element.

As the number of protons determines the element, you can also say that the nuclei of different elements have their own characteristic charge. In this example, a carbon nucleus always has a charge of +6.

6 protons
6 neutrons

6 protons
7 neutrons

6 protons
8 neutrons

● proton (atomic mass = 1)
● neutron (atomic mass = 1)
○ electron (atomic mass = 0)

Carbon atoms can contain different numbers of neutrons.

Worked example

The symbol represents an atom of sodium.

$^{23}_{11}Na$

Explain what these numbers tell you about the structure of the sodium nucleus. **(2 marks)**

The atomic number shows that sodium contains 11 protons. The mass number shows that it contains (23 − 11) = 12 neutrons.

Worked example

Explain how these atoms are similar and different:

$^{6}_{3}Li, \ ^{7}_{3}Li, \ ^{8}_{3}Li$ **(3 marks)**

They all contain the same number of protons and the same number of electrons (three of each). They have different numbers of neutrons, so they are different isotopes of lithium.

Now try this

1 Explain which two of these atoms are isotopes. **(2 marks)**

	Number of protons	Number of neutrons
Atom A	6	6
Atom B	6	7
Atom C	7	6

2 An atom of boron (B) has 5 protons and 6 neutrons. Show the atomic number and mass number as a symbol for the isotope. **(1 mark)**

Atoms, electrons and ions

Electrons can **move** between energy levels, or they can **leave** the atom completely.

Electrons in orbit

In all atoms, electrons orbit the nucleus in different orbits or energy levels, at different, fixed distances from the nucleus.

6 protons + 6 neutrons

⊖ electron
● neutron
⊕ proton

carbon atom

Moving between energy levels

An **electron** will move from a **lower to a higher orbit** if it **absorbs** electromagnetic radiation.

An **electron** will move from a **higher to a lower orbit** if it **emits** electromagnetic radiation.

electron

electromagnetic radiation

absorption   emission

Forming positive ions

Atoms become positively charged particles called **positive ions** when they **lose electrons**. There are now more protons present in the nucleus than there are electrons in the shells.

Electrons can leave an atom by:

① absorbing electromagnetic radiation of enough energy so that they can escape the pull of the nucleus; the three types of electromagnetic radiation that have enough energy to do that are UV, X-rays and gamma-rays;

② being hit by a particle such as an alpha particle or beta particle.

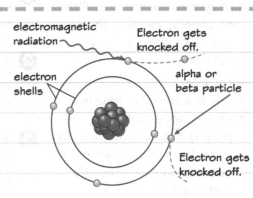

electromagnetic radiation
Electron gets knocked off.
electron shells
alpha or beta particle
Electron gets knocked off.

Worked example

State the overall charge of

(a) an atom   **(1 mark)**

neutral or 0

(b) a sodium atom that has lost an electron   **(1 mark)**

+1

(c) an atom where an electron has moved from a higher to lower orbit.   **(1 mark)**

neutral or 0

All atoms have a neutral overall charge. Positive ions are formed when an atom loses an electron.

Atoms can also gain electrons. They become negative ions with an overall negative charge.

No electron has been lost from the atom so there is no net change in the amount of charge present within the atom.

Now try this

1 State where
   (a) protons   **(1 mark)**
   (b) neutrons   **(1 mark)**
   (c) electrons   **(1 mark)**
   are found in atoms.

2 Explain how ions are different from atoms.
                                    (4 marks)

3 Determine what the overall charge of an atom would be if it:
   (a) lost two electrons   **(2 marks)**
   (b) gained one electron. **(2 marks)**

Ionising radiation

Alpha, **beta**, **gamma** and **neutron** radiation are **emitted** by **unstable nuclei**. The process is **random**, which means it is not possible to determine exactly **when** any nucleus will decay next.

Alpha, beta, gamma and neutron radiation

Some elements are **radioactive** because their nuclei are **unstable**. This means that they will undergo radioactive decay and change into other elements. Unstable nuclei will decay when alpha, beta, gamma or neutron radiation is emitted.

An **alpha particle** is a helium nucleus. It is composed of two protons and two neutrons. It has a charge of +2 and is the heaviest of

the particles emitted by unstable atoms. A **beta particle** is an electron. It has a charge of −1. A **positron** is an anti-electron and has a charge of +1.

A **gamma-ray** is a form of high-energy electromagnetic radiation. It has no mass or charge.

A **neutron** has zero charge.

Properties of radiation

Alpha and beta particles and gamma-rays can collide with atoms, ionising them by causing them to lose electrons.

Neutrons:
* are not directly ionising
* have a very high penetrating power due to them having no charge and not interacting strongly with matter

① (α) Alpha particles:
* will travel around 5 cm in air
* very ionising
* can be stopped by a sheet of paper.

② (β) Beta particles:
* will travel a few metres in air
* moderately ionising
* can be stopped by 3 mm thick aluminium.

③ (γ) Gamma-rays:
* will travel a few kilometres in air
* weakly ionising
* need thick lead to stop them.

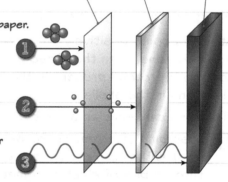

paper   aluminium   lead a few
        3 mm thick   cm thick

* can travel through humans and buildings for long distances before being stopped.

Worked example

Complete the table to show the properties of alpha, beta, gamma and neutron radiation.   **(5 marks)**

Type of radiation emitted	Relative charge	Relative mass	Ionising power	Penetrating power	Affected by magnetic fields?
alpha, α (helium nucleus, two protons and two neutrons)	+2	4	heavily ionising	very low, only ~5 cm in air	yes
beta, β− (an electron from the nucleus)	−1	1/1840	weakly ionising	low, stopped by thin aluminium	yes, but in the opposite direction to α and β+
positron, β+ (a particle with same size as electron but an opposite charge)	+1	1/1840	weakly ionising	low, stopped by thin aluminium	yes
neutron, n	0	1	not directly ionising	high	no, since neither are charged
gamma, γ (waves)	0	0	not directly ionising	very high, stopped only by thick lead	

Now try this

1 State which is the most ionising type of radiation.   **(1 mark)**

2 Explain why radioactive decay is a random process.   **(2 marks)**

Background radiation

Low levels of radiation are present around you all the time. This radiation is both **natural** and **man-made** and is called **background radiation**.

Background radiation

We are always exposed to ionising radiation. This is called **background radiation**. This radiation comes from different sources, as shown in the pie chart.

Radon is a radioactive gas that is produced when **uranium** in rocks decays. Radon decays by emitting an alpha particle. The radon can build up in houses and other buildings. The amount of radon gas varies from place to place, because it depends on the type of rock in the area.

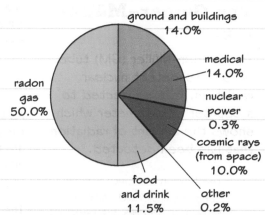

ground and buildings 14.0%
medical 14.0%
nuclear power 0.3%
cosmic rays (from space) 10.0%
other 0.2%
food and drink 11.5%
radon gas 50.0%

---

up to 1%
1–2.99%
3–4.99%
5–9.99%
10–29.99%
30% and over

Norfolk

Cornwall

Percentage of houses where radon is a potential problem.

Worked example

Give two examples of background radiation that are:
(a) naturally occurring **(2 marks)**

Cosmic rays and radioactivity from the ground.

(b) from human activities. **(2 marks)**

Nuclear power and medical, e.g. hospitals.

Naturally occurring background radiation comes from the environment around you such as the **soil, rocks, food, drink** and **cosmic rays** from outer space.

The artificial sources from human activities come from nuclear power stations, nuclear weapons and from departments in medical settings, such as hospitals, where radioactive materials are made and used.

Now try this

1 Which one of these is a source of artificial background radiation?

☐ **A** soil
☐ **B** rock
☐ **C** cosmic rays
☐ **D** medical X-rays   **(1 mark)**

2 Explain what is meant by the term background radiation. **(3 marks)**

3 Look at the map above. How would the pie chart above change if you lived in
(a) Norfolk
(b) Cornwall? **(2 marks)**

Measuring radioactivity

Photographic film and a **Geiger–Müller tube** can both be used to **measure** and **detect** radiation.

The Geiger–Müller tube

The Geiger–Müller (GM) tube is used to detect nuclear radiation. It is connected to a counter or ratemeter which shows the amount of radiation that has been detected.

> The text in red shows what is happening inside the GM tube, but you do not need to remember this in detail.

The GM tube contains argon gas. When radiation enters the tube, the atoms of argon are ionised and electrons travel towards the thin wire.

source Am-241

The GM tube has a thin wire in the middle which is connected to a voltage of +400 V.

As the electrons travel towards the thin wire, more electrons are knocked from atoms and an avalanche effect occurs.

The amount of radiation detected is shown by the ratemeter.

ratemeter

Detecting radiation

In 1896, Henri Becquerel discovered that uranium salts would lead to the darkening of a photographic film, even if it was wrapped up so that no light could reach it.

Radiation was being emitted from the uranium nuclei and this was responsible for the darkening of the film. This is now made use of in the nuclear industry as workers will wear a film badge to determine if they are being exposed to different forms of nuclear radiation.

photographic film inside

thin and thick plastic windows or aluminium – stop some beta particles

open window

lead between the plastic case and the film – stops beta and most gamma radiation

This dosimeter is a film badge used to monitor the radiation received by its wearer.

Worked example

(a) Explain why there is an open window in the film badge. **(3 marks)**

Light rays will darken the film. Since the film badge is designed to detect nuclear radiation, this acts as a control so that you know that the film is working.

(b) Explain why the film badge has aluminium and lead sheets inserted in it. **(3 marks)**

Aluminium absorbs beta particles and lead absorbs gamma-rays. If there is darkening behind these sheets, then high-energy beta- or gamma-rays may have got through and so the nature of the radiation can be determined and the risk identified.

> You should use your knowledge of the penetrating powers of the different types of radioactivity to answer the question.

Now try this

1 State the two types of device that are used to detect and measure radiation. **(2 marks)**

2 The photographic film behind the lead sheet darkens in the film badge worn by a worker in a nuclear power plant. Explain why the worker is concerned. **(3 marks)**

Models of the atom

The **model of the atom** has changed over time, based on **evidence** of its structure that became available from **experiments**.

Plum pudding model

J. J. Thomson's model of the atom was that the atom was like a 'plum pudding' with negatively charged 'electron plums' embedded in a uniform, positively charged 'dough' – a bit like the way currants look in a Christmas pudding.

This model showed that both positive and negative charges existed in atoms and accounted for the atom being neutral.

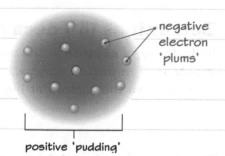

plum pudding model of the atom

Rutherford's model

Rutherford proposed that the atom must contain a very **small, positively charged nucleus** which electrons orbit – a bit like planets orbiting the Sun.

Rutherford's hypothesis was proved to be correct by Geiger and Marsden, who fired alpha particles at gold film.

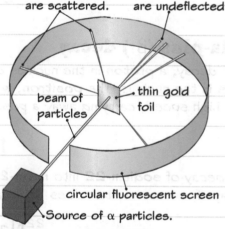

Rutherford scattering

The Bohr model

Niels Bohr showed that **electrons** had to orbit a **positive nucleus** in well-defined **energy levels** or orbits, but could move between energy levels if they gained or lost energy.

Worked example

Which model of the atom is being described?

(a) The atom is mostly empty space and has a positive nucleus which contains most of the mass of the atom. **(1 mark)**

Rutherford's model

(b) Electrons can only orbit the atom in certain energy levels or orbits. **(1 mark)**

the Bohr model of the atom

(c) The atom is neutral with negative 'plums' embedded in a positive 'dough'. **(1 mark)**

the plum pudding model

Now try this

Refer to page 41 for more information on electron levels.

1 Describe the three models of the atom. **(3 marks)**

2 Explain how Rutherford's work led to the conclusion that the atom had a small, positive nucleus. **(4 marks)**

3 Explain how new models of the atom become accepted over time. **(3 marks)**

Beta decay

One way in which unstable nuclei can undergo radioactive decay is by **beta decay**. There are two types – one where an **electron is emitted**, the other where a **positron is emitted**.

Beta-minus (β⁻) decay

In β⁻ decay, a **neutron** in the nucleus of an unstable atom decays to become a **proton** and an **electron**. The proton stays within the nucleus, but the **electron**, which is the β⁻ **particle**, is emitted from the nucleus at high speed as a fast-moving electron.

$$n \longrightarrow p + e^-$$

The decay of **carbon-14** into **nitrogen-14** by the emission of a β⁻ particle is an example of β⁻ decay. The mass number does not change, but the proton number **increases** by 1.

$$^{14}_{6}C \longrightarrow ^{14}_{7}N + ^{0}_{-1}e$$

Beta-plus (β+) decay

In β⁺ decay, a **proton** in the nucleus decays to become a **neutron** and a **positron**. The neutron stays in the nucleus. The **positron**, which is the β⁺ **particle**, is emitted from the nucleus at a very high speed, carrying away a positive charge and a very small amount of the nuclear mass.

$$p \longrightarrow n + e^+$$

The decay of **sodium-22** into **neon-22** by the emission of a positron is an example of β⁺ decay. The mass number does not change, but the proton number **decreases** by 1.

$$^{22}_{11}Na \longrightarrow ^{22}_{10}Ne + ^{0}_{+1}\beta$$

Worked example

Complete each equation and state whether it is β⁻ or β⁺ decay:

(a) $^{131}_{53}I \rightarrow ^{131}_{54}Xe + ?$ **(2 marks)**

Add $^{0}_{-1}e$. β⁻ decay

(b) $^{23}_{12}Mg \rightarrow ^{23}_{11}Na + ?$ **(2 marks)**

Add $^{0}_{1}e$. β⁺ decay

Uses of beta decay

Carbon-14 is an unstable isotope of carbon and emits β⁻ particles – it has a half-life of over 5700 years. This means that it can be used for radiocarbon dating, which involves finding the ages of materials that are thousands of years old. Positrons can be used in hospitals to form images of patients by the use of PET scans.

Now try this

1 Describe the changes that take place in the nucleus when it undergoes:
   (a) β⁻ decay   **(2 marks)**
   (b) β⁺ decay.   **(2 marks)**

2 Describe how a β⁻ particle is different from an electron that is found in a stable atom.   **(2 marks)**

3 Fill in the missing numbers in the decay equation and state the type of decay.   **(2 marks)**

$$^{66}_{28}Ni \rightarrow ^{-}_{29}Cu + ^{0}_{-}e$$

Radioactive decay

When unstable nuclei decay, the changes that occur depend on the **radiation** that is emitted from the **nucleus**.

Changes to the nucleus

Type of radiation	Effect on the mass of the nucleus	Effect on the charge of the nucleus
alpha α	nuclear mass reduced by 4 [−4]	positive charge reduced by 2 [−2]
beta $\beta-$	no change [0]	positive charge increased by 1 [+1]
beta $\beta+$	no change [0]	positive charge reduced by 1 [−1]
gamma	no effect on either the mass or the charge of a nucleus	
neutron	mass reduced by 1	no change of nuclear charge

Balancing nuclear decay equations

In any nuclear decay, the total mass and charge of the nucleus are conserved – they are the same before and after the decay. So the masses and charges on each side of the equation must balance.

When uranium-238 undergoes alpha decay, mass and charge are conserved. Nuclei that have undergone radioactive decay also undergo a rearrangement of their protons and neutrons. This involves the loss of energy from the nucleus in the form of gamma radiation. The mass and charge of the gamma-ray must be zero for the equation to balance:

$$\underset{\text{uranium}}{^{238}_{92}U} \longrightarrow \underset{\text{thorium}}{^{234}_{90}Th} + \underset{\substack{\text{alpha}\\\text{particle}}}{^{4}_{2}\alpha} + \underset{\substack{\text{gamma-}\\\text{ray}}}{\gamma}$$

When neutron decay occurs, mass and charge are also conserved:

$$^{13}_{4}Be \longrightarrow {^{12}_{4}Be} + {^{1}_{0}n}$$

Neutron decay results in another isotope of the same element being formed.

When beryllium decays by neutron emission, the mass and charge are both conserved. The nuclear charge will be +4 on both sides of the decay equation and the total mass will be 13.

Worked example

Balance the nuclear equations for these decays:

(a) Iodine-121 undergoes β^+ decay to form tellurium. **(2 marks)**

$^{121}_{53}I \rightarrow {^{121}_{52}Te} + {^{0}_{+1}e}$

> $^{0}_{+1}e$ is the emitted β^+ particle.

(b) An isotope of carbon undergoes β^- decay to form nitrogen-14. **(2 marks)**

$^{14}_{6}C \rightarrow {^{14}_{7}N} + {^{0}_{-1}e}$

> $^{0}_{-1}e$ is the emitted β^- particle.

(c) Radon-220 undergoes α decay to form an isotope of polonium. **(2 marks)**

$^{220}_{86}Rn \rightarrow {^{216}_{84}Po} + {^{4}_{2}He}$

> $^{4}_{2}He$ is the emitted α particle.

Now try this

1 Balance the nuclear equations for these decays and state the type of decay.

(a) $^{-}_{6}C \rightarrow {^{10}_{-}B} + {^{0}_{1}e}$ **(2 marks)**

(b) $^{232}_{-}Th \rightarrow {^{-}_{88}Ra} + {^{4}_{-}He}$ **(2 marks)**

2 A uranium nucleus contains 92 protons and 146 neutrons.

(a) State the mass number and atomic number of this uranium isotope. **(3 marks)**

(b) Determine what the mass number and atomic number will be if this uranium atom emits two alpha particles and a beta⁻ particle. **(4 marks)**

Half-life

The **activity** of a radioactive source is the number of atoms that **decay** every second. The unit for activity is the **becquerel (Bq)**. When an atom decays it emits radiation but changes into a more stable isotope.

Unstable atoms

The activity of a source depends on how many **unstable** atoms there are in a sample, and on the particular isotope. As more and more atoms in a sample decay, there are fewer unstable ones left, so the activity decreases. The **half-life** of a radioactive isotope is the time it takes for **half** of the **unstable** atoms to **decay**. This is also the time for the activity to go down by half.

We cannot predict when a particular nucleus will decay. But when there is a very large number of nuclei, the half-life gives a good prediction of the proportion of nuclei that will decay in a given time.

Radioactive decay and half-life

The number of radioactive nuclei present in a sample will halve after each successive half-life. After 1 half-life there will be 50% of the radioactive atoms left; after 2 half-lives there will be 25% of the radioactive atoms left, and so on.

Half-life example

The activity of a radioactive source is 240 Bq and its half-life is 6 hours.

After 1 half-life, the activity will halve to 120 Bq.

After 2 half-lives it will halve again to 60 Bq.

After 3 half-lives it will halve again to 30 Bq.

After 4 half-lives (one day) it will be 15 Bq.

Maths skills

Be careful when multiplying fractions:

After **1 half-life**, $\frac{1}{2}$ of the initial radioactive atoms are left.

After **2 half-lives**, $\frac{1}{2} \times \frac{1}{2}$ or $\frac{1}{4}$ are left.

After **3 half-lives**, $\frac{1}{2} \times \frac{1}{2} \times \frac{1}{2}$ or $\frac{1}{8}$ are left.

Worked example

The graph shows how the activity of a sample changes over 24 hours. What is the half-life of the sample? **(3 marks)**

Activity at time 0 = 1000 Bq

Half of this is 500 Bq. The activity is 500 Bq at 8 hours.

The half-life is 8 hours.

As the activity of a radioactive source decreases, the gradient of the graph will get less and less steep.

Now try this

1 The half-life of a radioactive source with an initial activity of 4000 Bq is known to be 2 days. Calculate the activity of the source after
  (a) 2 days   **(2 marks)**
  (b) 4 days   **(2 marks)**
  (c) 8 days.   **(2 marks)**

2 The activity of a source is 120 Bq. Four hours later it is found to be 30 Bq. Calculate the half-life of the source.
   (2 marks)

3 The half-life of a source is 15 minutes. Calculate the fraction that will remain after one hour. **(3 marks)**

Uses of radiation

The **uses** of alpha and beta particles and gamma-rays depend on their **properties**.

Uses of gamma rays

Radiation is used in hospitals to:

- **kill cancer cells** – beams of gamma-rays can be directed at cancer cells to kill them.
- **sterilise surgical instruments** – gamma-rays can be used to sterilise plastic instruments which cannot be sterilised by heating.
- **diagnose cancer** – a **tracer** solution containing a radioactive isotope that emits gamma-rays is injected into the body and taken up by cells which are growing abnormally. The places in the body where the tracer collects are detected with a 'gamma camera'.
- **preserve food** – food irradiated with gamma-rays will last longer as microbes are killed by the high-energy gamma-rays. The food does not become radioactive.

Smoke alarms

Smoke alarms contain a source of **alpha particles**.

Smoke enters the smoke detector.

Alpha particles ionise the air and these charged particles move across the gap forming a current.

Smoke in the machine will absorb alpha particles and make the current fall.

americium-241 alpha source

Siren will sound when the current falls.

Americium-241 source gives off a constant stream of alpha particles.

detector

A detector senses the amount of current.

Controlling thickness

If the paper is too thick, not as many beta particles get through.

→ The rollers press together harder to make the paper thinner or move apart to make it thicker.

detector   processor unit   hydraulic control

β radiation source

beta particles being used to control the thickness of paper

Worked example

Explain why beta particles are used to control the thickness of paper. **(3 marks)**

Alpha particles would not go through the paper at all. Gamma-rays would pass through the paper too easily, and the amount getting through would hardly change with small changes in the thickness of the paper.

Now try this

1 State three uses of ionising radiation.   **(3 marks)**

2 Explain why the radiation in smoke alarms is not dangerous to people in homes.   **(3 marks)**

3 Explain why ionising radiation is used to sterilise some equipment.   **(2 marks)**

Dangers of radiation

Ionising radiation can knock electrons out of atoms, turning the atoms into **ions**. This can be very **harmful** to humans.

Ionisation and cellular mutation

The energy transferred by ionising radiation can remove electrons from atoms to form **ions**. Ions are very reactive and can cause mutations to the **DNA** in **cells**. This can lead to **cancer**.

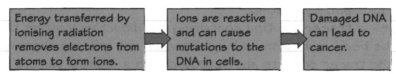

Energy transferred by ionising radiation removes electrons from atoms to form ions. → Ions are reactive and can cause mutations to the DNA in cells. → Damaged DNA can lead to cancer.

Ionising radiation can also cause damage to cell tissue in the form of radiation burns. When its energy is high enough it can also kill cells.

Precautions and safety

People who come into contact with ionising radiation need to be protected. They are protected by:

1. **limiting the time of exposure** – keep the time that a person needs to be in contact with the ionising radiation as **low** as possible

2. **wearing protective clothing** – wearing a **lead apron** will **absorb** much of the ionising radiation

3. **increasing the distance from the person to the radioactive source** – the **further** a person is from the ionising radiation, the **less damage** it will do.

To determine how much radiation a person has been exposed to, a film badge may be worn. See page 44 for more details.

The **greater the half-life** of an ionising source, the **longer** it will remain **dangerous**.

Precautions

People using radioactive material take precautions to make sure they stay safe.

radioactive source

The radioactive source is being moved using tongs to keep it as far away from the person's hand as possible. The source is always kept pointing away from people.

Worked example

Describe two precautions taken by dentists and dental nurses to reduce their exposure to ionising radiation while taking an X-ray. **(2 marks)**

1. They go out of the room in which the X-ray is taking place.

2. They keep the X-ray pulse as short as possible. (This also minimises the patient's exposure.)

The amount of energy that the human body is exposed to from a radioactive source is referred to as the **dose**. The dose needs to be big enough to obtain the X-ray image, but low enough to be safe for the patient and the dentist.

Now try this

1 State two ways in which ionising radiation can be dangerous to humans. **(2 marks)**

2 Explain why ionising radiation is more dangerous than non-ionising radiation. **(3 marks)**

3 Describe how people who work with radioactive materials decrease the risk of being exposed to high levels of ionising radiation. **(3 marks)**

Contamination and irradiation

You may be exposed to the effects of radioactive materials by being **irradiated** or **contaminated**.

Irradiation

Irradiation is ionising radiation from an external radioactive source travelling to the body – it is not breathed in, eaten or drunk.

Irradiation does not refer to non-harmful rays from televisions, light bulbs or other non-ionising sources.

Alpha particles are unlikely to be harmful outside the body as they have a very short range in air (5 cm) and are unlikely to reach a person.

Irradiation is the exposure of a person to ionising radiation from outside the body. This could be in the form of harmful gamma-rays, beta particles or X-rays.

When ionising radiation reaches the body, cells may be damaged or killed, but you will not become radioactive.

Contamination

External contamination occurs when radioactive materials **come into contact with a person's hair, skin or clothing**.

Internal contamination occurs when a radioactive source is eaten or drunk. Some nuts, plants, fruits and alcoholic drinks have low levels of radioactivity. This is due to the radioactive minerals that they are exposed to during their growth or manufacture.

Remember that with contamination, the radioactive source comes into contact with the skin or is taken into the body. This can be through the mouth or nose, or through a cut in the skin. With irradiation, the source does not come into contact with the skin.

Worked example

State what type of contamination the following examples are describing:
(a) eating radioactive strontium-90 that is found in some foods **(1 mark)**
internal contamination
(b) being exposed to cosmic rays from the Sun **(1 mark)**
irradiation
(c) having an X-ray to find if a bone is broken **(1 mark)**
irradiation
(d) radioactive dust comes into contact with the skin. **(1 mark)**
external contamination

Now try this

1 Define
(a) irradiation **(2 marks)**
(b) contamination. **(2 marks)**

2 Explain why alpha particles are more likely to cause damage inside the body rather than outside the body. **(3 marks)**
3 Describe how background radiation is a mixture of contamination and irradiation. **(2 marks)**

Medical uses

Ionising radiation can be used **internally** and **externally** to **diagnose illnesses** and **treat cancer.**

Medical tracers

Medical tracers are substances that are used in **biological** processes in the body and contain a **radioisotope**.

The patient can **eat** or **drink** this substance, or it can be **injected** into the body.

The **ionising radiation** emitted by the tracer can be **detected** and the biological process **monitored**. Doctors can diagnose the nature and location of any health problems.

For example, **fluorodeoxyglucose (FDG)** is a radioactive form of glucose that is commonly used as a tracer. Once it is in the blood it travels to the tissues that use glucose. When part of the brain is affected, **less radioactivity** is detected because glucose is not being used.

PET scanners

PET scanners are used to produce 3D colour images of the internal workings of the patient.

1. The **tracer** is a radioactive material that decays quickly by emitting positrons.

2. When these positrons come into contact with electrons in the body, the two particles **annihilate** each other, resulting in the formation of **gamma-rays**.

3. These gamma rays are detected by the **PET scanner** and processed by a computer, and an image is then displayed on a computer screen.

4. As the tracers **decay quickly**, they need to be produced close to where they are used.

Treating tumours internally

Cancer tumours can be treated internally by using a radioactive source that is inside the patient. The source enters the patient by:

1. **injecting** the radioisotope into the patient

2. the patient **eating** or **drinking** something which contains the radioisotope in solid or liquid form.

In the treatment of thyroid cancer, the radioactive element iodine-131 is used. It is swallowed in a capsule. The iodine is taken up by the thyroid gland but not by other parts of the body. This means that the ionising radiation is likely to kill the thyroid cancer without affecting other healthy cells surrounding it.

Treating tumours externally

1. Several beams of gamma rays are fired, from different positions, towards the cancer.

2. Each beam is not energetic enough to kill the tumour, but damages it.

3. By moving the beam, the amount of ionising radiation received by the surrounding tissue is reduced.

source of gamma-rays

gamma-rays

target

Worked example

Explain why internal treatments are used to treat cancer tumours. **(3 marks)**

When internal treatments are used, the ionising radiation can be targeted at the tumour. This means that most of the ionising radiation goes to the tumour and damage to surrounding areas is reduced. With external treatment, the ionising radiation has to pass through healthy tissue which can be damaged.

Now try this

1 Define what a medical tracer is. **(2 marks)**

2 Explain why several low-energy gamma-ray beams are used instead of a single high-energy beam when treating cancer with gamma-rays from an external source. **(4 marks)**

3 Explain why gamma rays are used as medical tracers instead of other types of radiation. **(3 marks)**

Nuclear power

Electrical energy can be generated in power stations that use **nuclear fuel**. There are advantages and disadvantages of nuclear power.

Energy from the nucleus

All nuclear reactions can be a source of energy:

1. **Radioactive decay:** can be in the form of alpha or beta particles, or gamma rays (which are electromagnetic waves).

2. **Nuclear fusion:** the fusing of hydrogen nuclei in the Sun releases enormous amounts of light and heat, some of which we receive on Earth.

3. **Nuclear fission:** uranium nuclei are split by slow-moving neutrons in a nuclear reactor, resulting in the release of enormous amounts of thermal energy.

Nuclear power and waste

Nuclear power is a **highly efficient** way of producing electrical energy. Much less nuclear fuel is needed, compared with coal, oil or gas, to produce the same amount of electrical energy. However, nuclear power stations do produce radioactive **nuclear waste**, which needs to be dealt with. Some of it is radioactive for thousands of years.

Nuclear power

There are advantages and disadvantages to using nuclear energy to generate electricity.

👍 Nuclear power stations do not produce **carbon dioxide**, so they do not contribute to climate change.

👍 Supplies of nuclear fuel will **last longer** than supplies of fossil fuels.

However, construction processes produce carbon dioxide, so carbon dioxide will be added to the atmosphere when the power station is built and when fuel rods are made.

👎 It is difficult and expensive to **store** nuclear waste safely.

👎 An **accident** in a nuclear power station can spread **radioactive material** over a large area.

👎 Many people think that nuclear power is dangerous, and do not want new nuclear power stations to be built.

Nuclear power stations do not make the local area more radioactive when they are working properly. This only happens if there is an accident.

Worked example

Explain the disadvantages of nuclear power.　**(3 marks)**

Nuclear radiation is very dangerous, so a nuclear accident could kill many people. There is much radioactive waste which is difficult and expensive to store, and some of it is radioactive for many thousands of years. Public perception surrounding nuclear power as a form of energy means that people often distrust it because of previous accidents such as at Chernobyl and Fukushima.

Despite the problems, it is important to remember that nuclear power has some real advantages, including the fact that no carbon dioxide is produced when a power station is in operation (and so they do not affect climate change) and that the fuel supplies will last longer than coal, oil or gas reserves.

Now try this

1　'Nuclear power does not produce carbon dioxide emissions.'
　Explain why this statement is not correct.　　　　　　　　　　**(3 marks)**
2　Describe how nuclear power pollutes the environment.　　　　　**(4 marks)**

Nuclear fission

The fission of uranium-235 results in the **release of a large quantity of energy**, which is then used to **heat water** in power stations.

Nuclear fission

In a **fission reaction**, a large unstable nucleus splits into two smaller ones. For example, a **uranium-235** nucleus splits up when it absorbs a **neutron**. The fission of uranium-235 produces two **daughter nuclei**, two or more neutrons, and also releases energy. The daughter nuclei are also radioactive.

Controlled chain reactions

Two of the neutrons are absorbed by other materials. Only one neutron from each fission can cause another fission. This is a **controlled chain reaction**.

Chain reactions

The neutrons released by the fission of U-235 may be absorbed by other nuclei. Each of these nuclei may undergo fission, and produce even more neutrons. This is called a **chain reaction**. If a chain reaction is not controlled there will be a nuclear explosion.

Nuclear reactors make use of **controlled chain reactions** (see next page).

Worked example

Describe how a chain reaction can be controlled.
(3 marks)

A chain reaction can be controlled by using a different material to absorb some of the neutrons. This slows the reaction down because there are fewer neutrons to cause more nuclei to undergo fission.

Now try this

1 Describe what happens in the fission of uranium-235.   **(3 marks)**
2 Describe the difference between a chain reaction and a controlled chain reaction.   **(4 marks)**
3 Explain why:
   (a) neutrons in a nuclear reaction need to be slow moving   **(2 marks)**
   (b) only one neutron should be absorbed by a uranium-235 nucleus.   **(2 marks)**

Nuclear power stations

You need to know how electricity can be generated from **nuclear fission** in nuclear power stations.

Generating electrical energy from nuclear fission

It is the thermal energy from nuclear fission that is most useful for the generation of electricity in a power station.

3 The steam causes turbines to rotate which turn the generator to generate electricity.

1 Fuel rods containing uranium undergo nuclear fission. Thermal energy is released.

2 A coolant such as water is pumped through the reactor. Thermal energy from nuclear fission is taken by the coolant to heat water to produce steam.

4 The steam is cooled back into water in a condenser so it can be used again. Extra thermal energy is released from cooling towers, or into the sea.

Controlling the chain reaction

Concrete shielding prevents radiation and stray neutrons escaping from the core.

Control rods absorb neutrons.

Neutrons that escape from one fuel rod can be absorbed by another.

Lowering a control rod reduces fission reactions.

A moderator is a material (often graphite or water) that is used to slow down the neutrons so that fission of the uranium-235 nuclei can occur. The moderator does not absorb neutrons.

Explain how the control rods work in a nuclear power station. **(3 marks)**

The control rods **absorb** neutrons. If the control rods are pushed down into the core, more neutrons are absorbed and the chain reaction slows down. If they are pulled out, fewer neutrons are absorbed and the chain reaction speeds up.

(a) Describe how nuclear fuel is used in a power station. **(2 marks)**

Nuclear fuel undergoes fission to release huge quantities of thermal energy. This is used to heat water to produce steam.

(b) Describe what happens to the products of nuclear fission. **(2 marks)**

The radioactive daughter products need to be disposed of safely. They are usually stored until the activity has decreased to a safe level.

1 (a) Describe one **advantage** of using nuclear fuel compared with fossil fuels. **(1 mark)**

(b) Describe one **disadvantage** of using nuclear fuel compared with fossil fuels. **(1 mark)**

2 Explain how pulling control rods out of the core of a nuclear reactor can increase the amount of thermal energy released by the reactor. **(4 marks)**

Nuclear fusion

Nuclear fusion involves the **joining of smaller nuclei** to form **larger nuclei**. Obtaining a continuous supply of energy from nuclear fusion is **more difficult** than obtaining energy from nuclear fission.

Nuclear fusion

Nuclear **fusion** happens when small nuclei join to form larger ones. Like all nuclear reactions, fusion reactions **release energy**.

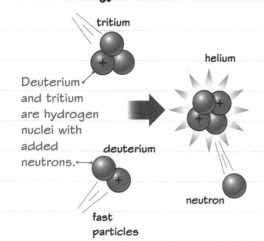

tritium

helium

Deuterium and tritium are hydrogen nuclei with added neutrons.

deuterium

neutron

fast particles

Fusion and stars

During the stable period of a star's life, vast quantities of hydrogen nuclei are converted to helium nuclei by nuclear fusion. This is the source of energy for stars.

Over time, heavier elements are formed and the star will eventually die. This will take our Sun billions of years. One of the typical reactions that takes place in the Sun is:

$$_1^2H + {}_1^3H \longrightarrow {}_2^4He + {}_0^1n + energy$$

The mass of the products is slightly less than the mass of the reactants – this mass difference is released as energy in the form of thermal energy.

This reaction takes place under very high pressure and temperature in stars.

Difficulties of fusion

Nuclei need to get very close to each other before fusion can happen. Under normal conditions the positive charges on nuclei repel each other. This is called **electrostatic repulsion**. Only at very high temperatures and pressures are the nuclei moving fast enough for them to overcome this electrostatic repulsion.

The very high temperatures and pressures needed are very difficult to produce in a fusion power station. All the experimental fusion reactors built so far have used more energy than they have produced!

Worked example

Explain the difference between nuclear fusion and nuclear fission.   **(3 marks)**

In nuclear fusion hydrogen nuclei fuse to produce helium nuclei whereas in nuclear fission uranium-235 splits into two smaller nuclei and two or three neutrons.

Nuclear fusion requires very high temperatures and pressures whereas nuclear fission requires a slow-moving neutron to be absorbed.

Both processes release large quantities of energy.

Fusion can occur in the Sun and other stars because the enormous temperatures and pressures allow the charged nuclei to overcome the repulsive electrostatic forces between them.

Now try this

1 Describe what happens during nuclear fusion.   **(3 marks)**
2 Describe how the processes of fusion and fission release energy.   **(3 marks)**
3 Explain why there are no commercial power stations using fusion reactions.   **(3 marks)**

Extended response – Radioactivity

There will be one or more 6-mark questions on your exam paper. For these questions, you will need to think scientifically and structure your answer logically, showing how the points you make are related to each other. You can revise the topics for this question, which is about **radioactivity**, on pages 39–56.

Worked example

Unstable nuclei emit **ionising** radiation which can cause damage to human tissue.

Explain the precautions that need to be taken to reduce the potential danger of ionising radiation to humans.

Your answer should refer to the nature of ionising radiation and how it may be dangerous both inside and outside the body.

(6 marks)

Ionising radiation is radiation that has enough energy to knock electrons from the outer shells of atoms, turning them from neutral atoms to positively charged ions. There are three types of ionising radiation that are emitted from the nucleus – alpha and beta particles and gamma rays. Alpha particles are the most ionising and gamma rays are the least ionising.

Since ionising radiation can damage human tissue and cause mutations in cells, leading to cancer, it is necessary to take precautions. These precautions include wearing lead aprons to absorb the radiation, being exposed to as low a radiation energy as possible, being as far from the radioactive source as possible and being exposed for as short a period of time as possible. All of these help to reduce the exposure to ionising radiation.

Inside the body, alpha particles are easily absorbed and can cause cellular mutations which can lead to cancer. Beta particles and gamma rays tend to pass out of the body. Alpha particles are not dangerous outside the body as they will not reach the body due to their short range, but beta particles and gamma rays can reach the body and can cause damage to cells.

Command words: Explain

When you are asked to **explain** something, it is not enough to just state or describe something. Your answer **must** contain some reasoning or justification of the points you make based on the physics being addressed. This needs to be communicated clearly with good spelling, punctuation, grammar and sentence structure.

The answer starts with an explanation of what ionising radiation is as well as a description of the three main types of ionising radiation and their relative ionising abilities.

The second paragraph addresses the dangers and the precautions that need to be taken to ensure that exposure does not lead to adverse health issues.

Contamination and irradiation

Although not mentioned here specifically in the answer, you could state that material emitting ionising radiation can be breathed into the body or eaten, in which case the person is **contaminated**, and that the radiation could reach them as beta particles or gamma rays from an external source, in which case the person is being **irradiated**.

The final paragraph looks at which type of radiation is most dangerous inside the body as well as which types of radiation are most dangerous when the radioactive source is outside the body.

Now try this

Describe how and why the atomic model has changed over time. Your answer should refer to three different models of the atom. **(6 marks)**

The Solar System

The **Solar System** contains the **Sun**, **eight planets**, their **natural satellites**, **dwarf planets**, **asteroids** and **comets**. Ideas about the structure of the Solar System have changed over time.

The Solar System

You need to remember the order of the eight planets, going from the Sun.

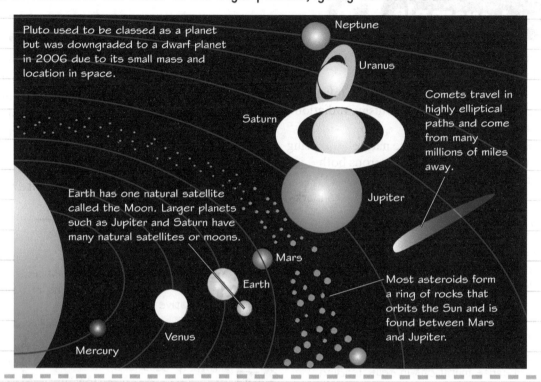

Pluto used to be classed as a planet but was downgraded to a dwarf planet in 2006 due to its small mass and location in space.

Neptune

Uranus

Saturn

Comets travel in highly elliptical paths and come from many millions of miles away.

Earth has one natural satellite called the Moon. Larger planets such as Jupiter and Saturn have many natural satellites or moons.

Jupiter

Mars

Earth

Most asteroids form a ring of rocks that orbits the Sun and is found between Mars and Jupiter.

Venus

Mercury

Changing ideas

Many early people thought that the **Sun** and all the **planets** moved around the Earth.

In about 130 CE a Greek astronomer called Ptolemy published a **geocentric** ('Earth-centred') model that tried to explain the motions of the planets.

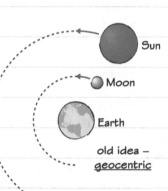

Sun

Moon

Earth

old idea – geocentric

In 1543 Nicolaus Copernicus published a book that argued that the Earth and the planets were in **orbits** around the Sun. This is a **heliocentric** ('Sun-centred') model.

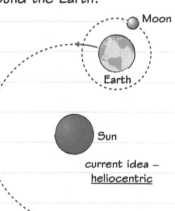

Moon

Earth

Sun

current idea – heliocentric

Worked example

 State what the Solar System is composed of. **(3 marks)**

The Solar System is composed of the Sun, eight planets, asteroids, comets and dwarf planets such as Pluto.

Now try this

1 State the difference between a geocentric and a heliocentric model of the Solar System. **(2 marks)**

2 Name the planets in order from the Sun, starting with the furthest. **(2 marks)**

3 Suggest why some planets have been discovered more recently than others. **(3 marks)**

You could make up a mnemonic to help you remember the order.

Satellites and orbits

Bodies of **lower mass** will travel in **orbits** around **bodies of much higher mass**. The nature of these orbits needs to be known for a variety of natural and artificial satellites.

Natural satellites

Natural satellites were formed by natural processes. Examples include:

- the eight **planets** in the Solar System which orbit the Sun
- the **moons** which orbit planets in the Solar System
- **comets** which orbit the Sun.

Artificial satellites

Artificial satellites are manufactured and have been launched into space from Earth by using rockets. Examples include:

- satellites in **geostationary orbits** around the Earth being used for global positioning satellite systems (GPS)
- satellites in **low polar orbits** around the Earth being used for weather monitoring, military, spying or Earth observation purposes
- satellites **sent from Earth** to orbit and monitor the Sun, other planets or asteroids in the Solar System.

Type of orbit

Artificial satellites orbiting the Earth, and planets orbiting the Sun, tend to move in circular or near-circular orbits.

Comets travel in highly elliptical orbits around the Sun.

The gravitational force of the Sun acting on the comet gets weaker as it gets further away from the Sun. The comet will travel more slowly when it is far from the Sun and faster when it is closer to the Sun.

Earth Sun
Jupiter
Saturn

R

comet orbit

The gravitational force acting on a body in a circular orbit will be the same at each point of the orbit, since the radius is fixed. The speed of the orbit will not change, but the velocity will be constantly changing because the direction is constantly changing.

The speed and velocity of a comet change constantly.

Worked example

Compare the motion of Earth, Jupiter and Saturn as they orbit the Sun. **(3 marks)**

All three planets travel in circular orbits and have a constant speed and a changing velocity. As the distance from the Sun increases, the orbital speed decreases. The Earth has a higher orbital speed than Jupiter which has a higher orbital speed than Saturn.

The planets in the Solar System are in stable orbits. For example:

1. If the Earth's orbital speed increased then the gravitational force from the Sun would not keep it in orbit. It would fly out of its orbit, into a new orbit of greater radius.

2. If the Earth's orbital speed decreased, the Sun's gravitational field would cause it to fall towards it, into a new orbit of smaller radius.

Now try this

1 State the nature of the speed and velocity of a body that is moving in a circular orbit. **(2 marks)**

2 Describe how the speed and velocity of a comet changes over the course of one orbit. **(4 marks)**

3 Describe what might happen to a GPS satellite if its orbital speed changed. **(4 marks)**

Theories about the Universe

Scientists' ideas about the **birth** and **evolution** of the **Universe** have changed over time.

Existence theories

There are two different **theories** about the Universe.

> The **Big Bang** theory says that the whole Universe started out as a tiny particle about **13.8 billion years** ago. The Universe expanded from this point in space. The Universe is still **expanding** today.

> The **Steady State** theory says that the Universe has always existed. It is expanding, and new matter is being created as it expands.

The Big Bang theory is currently the most accepted model, based on the available evidence.

Red-shift

When objects that emit light, such as galaxies, are moving away from us then the light they emit is 'red-shifted'. This means that the wavelengths from them when detected back on Earth will be 'stretched'. The spectral lines will be shifted further to the red end of the spectrum, compared with a stationary object observed on Earth. Also, the faster the galaxy is travelling away from us, the more these lines will be shifted to the red end of the spectrum. Since the furthest galaxies show more red shift than those nearer to us, this suggests that the Universe is expanding.

CMB

The CMB (**Cosmic Microwave Background**) radiation is the 'echo' of the Big Bang. At the time of the Big Bang, this radiation would have been incredibly hot and intense. Over time, the radiation has cooled and is now very weak and at a temperature of −270°C, close to absolute zero. The fact that the CMBR is detected in all directions and has the temperature that it does, is evidence that the Universe started with a Big Bang almost 14 billion years ago.

Worked example

Describe the cosmic microwave background radiation (CMBR) and explain why the Big Bang theory is the currently accepted model for the beginning of the Universe. **(4 marks)**

> Although red-shift is evidence for both the Steady State theory and the Big Bang theory, it is the cosmic microwave background radiation that provides the key evidence for the Big Bang theory.

The cosmic microwave background radiation is detected by radio telescopes and comes from all over the sky. The Big Bang theory says that this radiation was released at the beginning of the Universe.

Red-shift supports both the Big Bang and the Steady State theories, but the CMBR only supports the Big Bang theory. The Big Bang theory is accepted because it has the most evidence supporting it.

Now try this

 1 Name the two main theories about the Universe. **(2 marks)**

 2 Why is the cosmic microwave background radiation such important evidence? **(3 marks)**

 3 Three galaxies are at different distances from Earth. Explain how you would be able to tell which of these three galaxies was
(a) closest to Earth **(2 marks)**
(b) furthest away from Earth. **(2 marks)**

Doppler effect and red-shift

The **Doppler effect** and **red-shift** both provide **evidence** for the nature of the Universe.

The Doppler effect

When a wave source is moving relative to an observer, there is a change in the observed frequency and wavelength of the waves. Consider the siren in the car shown in the picture.

The driver of the car is not moving relative to the siren, so the pitch she hears is the same all the time, as it would be for an external observer if the car were stationary.

The car is currently travelling towards observer 2. This compresses the sound wave, making the frequency higher, and so the pitch of the siren sounds higher to observer 2.

The car is currently travelling away from observer 1. This stretches the sound wave out, giving it a longer wavelength (so a lower frequency). The pitch therefore sounds lower to observer 1.

observer 1   car travelling towards the right   observer 2

Red-shift and the Doppler effect

The Doppler effect occurs for light waves as well as for sound waves.

A light source moving away from an observer will have a **greater wavelength** and a **lower frequency**. It is 'red-shifted'.

A light source moving towards an observer will have a **smaller wavelength** and a **higher frequency**. It is 'blue-shifted'.

Red-shift and evidence for the expanding Universe

In 1929, the astronomer Edwin Hubble discovered that the light reaching Earth from galaxies was red-shifted. He found this out by looking at the spectral lines in the absorption spectra of stars that are moving away from us.

Galaxy B's lines are red-shifted the most, so it is moving away from us the fastest.

	blue	red
laboratory hydrogen spectral lines		
galaxy A spectral lines		
galaxy B spectral lines		

Worked example

Explain how red-shift suggests that the Universe is expanding. **(4 marks)**

The light received on Earth from most galaxies is red-shifted. This means that most galaxies are moving away from us. The furthest galaxies from us have the greatest red-shift, so are moving away from us faster. This suggests that the Universe is expanding.

Now try this

1 Describe an example of the Doppler effect for
 (a) sound waves **(2 marks)**
 (b) light waves. **(2 marks)**
2 Suggest how the speed of a galaxy can be determined from the absorption lines in its spectrum. **(3 marks)**

Life cycle of stars

Stars go through a number of **stages** in their lives. Their eventual **fate** depends on their **mass**.

Low-mass stars

The Sun was formed about 4.6 billion years ago and is nearly halfway through its life. Stars with masses up to four times the mass of the Sun are classified as low-mass stars.

1. The cloud of **dust** and **hydrogen gas** (a **nebula**), is pulled inwards by the force of gravity. As the dust and gas contracts the nebular gets hotter since work is being done on it.

2. Eventually, the dust and gas become hot enough for the hydrogen nuclei to fuse. **Nuclear fusion** leads to heavier **helium nuclei** being produced and large amounts of **energy** being released. The star will begin to give out **light** and is now a **main-sequence** star. Stars are main-sequence stars for most of their lives. The inwards force of gravity is balanced by the outwards force of thermal expansion.

3. When most of the hydrogen gas has been converted to helium, the star will **expand** and become a **red giant**. When the core of this star collapses, other **heavier elements** are formed.

4. Eventually, all nuclear fusion stops due to the elements that cause fusion being used up, and the star **collapses** to become a **white dwarf**.

High-mass stars

A star with a much higher mass than the Sun follows the same first stages of the life cycle, but each stage is shorter. When most of its hydrogen is used up it forms a **red supergiant**. At the end of this stage the star will explode as a **supernova**. If what remains after the explosion is less than four times the mass of the Sun it will be pulled together by gravity to form a very small, dense star called a **neutron star**. More massive remnants form **black holes**.

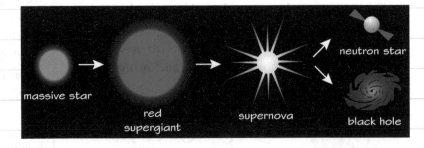

massive star — red supergiant — supernova — neutron star / black hole

Worked example

Explain how the fate of a low-mass star is different from that of a high-mass star. **(6 marks)**

A low-mass star will move off the main sequence and expand to become a red giant before cooling and contracting to become a white dwarf. A high-mass star will move off the main sequence, become a red supergiant and explode in a supernova. The mass that is left in the core will become a very dense neutron star or a black hole.

Now try this

1 State the stages in the life cycle of
   (a) low-mass stars **(4 marks)**
   (b) high-mass stars. **(4 marks)**

2 'The Sun will not become a neutron star or a black hole'. Explain why this statement is true. **(3 marks)**

3 Describe how the forces of gravity and thermal expansion play an important part in the life cycle of a star. **(4 marks)**

Observing the Universe

Methods used to observe the Universe have changed over time. Originally, observations were made **from Earth**. Now there are **telescopes in space** to observe the Universe from above the Earth's atmosphere.

Modern telescopes

The first scientists explored the Universe by observing the **visible light** emitted by stars. They made more discoveries after telescopes were invented. Modern telescopes are very different to the early telescopes.

Development	Impact
greater magnifications	We can observe galaxies that are far away.
recording observations using photography or digital cameras	We can gather more data.
can be made with greater precision	We get clearer images.
telescopes that can detect other parts of the electromagnetic spectrum	We can observe objects in space that emit more radio waves, infrared, ultraviolet or X-rays than visible light.

Observing the Universe from Earth and from space

Some parts of the electromagnetic spectrum are absorbed by the Earth's atmosphere. Telescopes used to observe these wavelengths of radiation must be put on satellites in space.

Ultraviolet telescopes need to be placed in orbit to detect ultraviolet radiation.

The radio waves in this range of wavelengths will reach us from space and be detected by radio telescopes on Earth. Longer wavelengths will not be detected.

Worked example

Use the diagram above to help with the answer.

Suggest why the cosmic microwave background radiation was detected on Earth.   **(2 marks)**

The longer wavelength microwaves that form the cosmic microwave background radiation are not absorbed by the Earth's atmosphere.

Now try this

 1 Name the two main places where telescopes can be placed.
(2 marks)

 2 Explain why visible light telescopes can be based on Earth or in space. **(4 marks)**

3 Explain how developments in modern telescopes have improved our knowledge of the Universe. **(4 marks)**

Extended response – Astronomy

There will be one or more 6-mark questions on your exam paper. For these questions, you will need to think scientifically and structure your answer logically, showing how the points you make are related to each other. You can revise the topics for this question, which is about **astronomy**, on pages 9 and 58–63.

Worked example

Astronomers collect data and use evidence to try to explain the origins of the Universe. For many years, there were two competing theories: the Steady State theory and the Big Bang theory.

Compare and contrast these theories.

Your answer should refer to the nature of any evidence which suggests that the Big Bang theory is the better theory. **(6 marks)**

The Big Bang theory states that the Universe started from a single, infinitely dense point in a massive explosion about 13.8 billion years ago and has been expanding and cooling ever since. The Steady State theory says that the Universe has always existed, and that it is also expanding.

The two key pieces of evidence for the Big Bang theory are the red-shift of galaxies and the cosmic microwave background radiation. Spectral lines in absorption spectra are shifted to the red end of the spectrum due to the stretching of light waves when galaxies move away from us. As the spectral lines from the majority of galaxies show red-shift, this suggests that the Universe is expanding. The cosmic microwave background radiation is the low-energy radiation or 'echo' of the Big Bang, at a temperature of 2.7 K, due to the cooling of gamma-rays that were emitted at the start of the Universe. The temperature of the cosmic microwave background radiation suggests that the Universe is the age that it has been predicted to be by the Big Bang theory.

The Big Bang theory is the more accepted theory because there is more evidence to support it as a theory for the Universe. Whilst the red-shift supports both theories, the cosmic microwave background radiation is strong evidence for the birth of the Universe in a Big Bang and not for a Steady State theory.

Command words: Compare and contrast

When you are asked to **compare and contrast**, you should describe the similarities and differences of both cases. You are not required to draw a conclusion.

When comparing and contrasting two theories you need to state how they are both similar and different. The main similarity and difference are stated here.

The two key pieces of evidence are stated and then described in more detail. The two pieces that need to be mentioned are red-shift and the cosmic microwave background radiation. There are other pieces of evidence, but stick with those mentioned on the specification.

Evidence is central to theories being accepted. You need to know what this evidence is so that you can explain why the Big Bang theory is the generally accepted one.

Decide what you are going to include in your answer, and plan the order of your answer before you start writing it. Think about the evidence you need to provide.

Now try this

Two stars are both in the main-sequence stage of their life. Describe what their possible fates could be and explain why these fates might be very different. **(6 marks)**

Work, energy and power

The **work** done by a force is the same as the **energy** transferred by the force. **Power** is the **rate of work** being done or the **rate at which energy is transferred**. You should already be familiar with some of the content about energy for this topic which is covered on pages 15, 16 and 18.

Work done and energy

Work done is the amount of energy transferred, and is measured in **joules (J)**.

Work done is calculated using this formula:

$$\underset{\text{(J)}}{\text{work done}} = \underset{\text{(N)}}{\text{force}} \times \underset{\substack{\text{distance moved in} \\ \text{the direction of the} \\ \text{force (m)}}}{}$$

$$E = F \times d$$

LEARN IT!
IT'S NOT ON THE EQUATIONS LIST

$$\frac{E}{F \times d}$$

You can measure the work done by recording the size of the force and the distance moved in the direction of the force. Multiply these values together to find the value for the work done.

Power

Power is the rate of doing work (how fast energy is transferred). Power is measured in **watts (W)**. 1 watt is 1 joule of energy being transferred every second.

$$\text{power (W)} = \frac{\text{work done (J)}}{\text{time taken (s)}}$$

$$P = \frac{E}{t}$$

LEARN IT!
IT'S NOT ON THE EQUATIONS LIST

$$\frac{E}{P \times t}$$

A hairdryer with a power of 1800 W transfers 1800 J each second.

Changing the energy of a system

The energy of a system can be changed by:

1 **work done through forces:** a body can be lifted through a vertical height by a force. This will increase the store of gravitational potential energy.

2 **electrical equipment:** a cell in a circuit provides a potential difference so that components in the circuit can transfer energy into other forms, such as thermal energy.

3 **heating a material:** supplying thermal energy to a system will increase the kinetic energy of the particles in the material. Its temperature will increase if it is not changing state.

Worked example

(a) Dan uses a force of 100 N to push a box across the floor. He pushes it for 3 m. Calculate the work done. **(3 marks)**

Work done = 100 N × 3 m = 300 J

(b) A kettle converts 360 000 J of electrical energy into thermal energy in 3 minutes whilst heating a mass of water. Calculate the power of the kettle. **(3 marks)**

Power = energy ÷ time

= 360 000 J ÷ (3 × 60 s) = 2000 W

Don't get work and power mixed up. Remember:

Work = energy transferred, measured in joules.

Power = **rate** of energy transfer, measured in watts.

Always make sure that energy is in J and time is in s before substituting to find an answer in W.

Now try this

1 Calculate how much work is done when 350 N pushes an object through 30 m along the floor.
(3 marks)

2 Calculate how much energy an 1800 W hairdryer transfers when used for 8 minutes.
(3 marks)

3 Calculate the power of a light bulb that transfers 3600 J of energy in one minute.
(3 marks)

Extended response – Energy and forces

There will be one or more 6-mark questions on your exam paper. For these questions, you will need to think scientifically and structure your answer logically, showing how the points you make are related to each other. You can revise the topics for this question, which is about **energy and forces**, on pages 15, 16 and 65.

Worked example

You can find more information on efficiency on page 16.

Energy stores and energy transfers can be shown on energy transfer diagrams.

An energy transfer diagram is shown for a battery-operated fan.

Explain how this energy transfer diagram can be used to determine the efficiency of the fan.

Your answer should refer to the term efficiency, the equation for efficiency and a calculation. **(6 marks)**

For the energy transfer diagram shown, the input is in the form of a chemical energy store, which is transferred to kinetic energy, sound energy and thermal energy.

For the energy transfer diagram shown, for every 100 J of energy transferred from the chemical energy store of the battery, there will be 56 J transferred to the kinetic energy, 17 J to the thermal energy store in the surroundings and 27 J to the thermal energy store in the motor.

Since a battery-operated fan is designed to transfer the chemical energy store to kinetic energy as a useful form, 56 J of the 100 J of chemical energy can be deemed to be useful, and 44 J can be assumed to be wasted.

The efficiency of a device is the proportion of the input energy that is usefully transferred and is calculated using the equation:

$$\text{Efficiency} = \frac{(\text{useful output energy})}{(\text{total input energy})} \times 100\%$$

For the battery-operated fan, the efficiency is 56 J ÷ 100 J × 100% which is an efficiency of 56%.

The answer starts by simply stating what the energy transfer diagram is showing in terms of energy stores and transfers.

This part of the answer explains which energy store is useful as an output energy store and which of the stores are wasted energy stores. It also states the amounts that are useful and wasted.

Command word: Explain

When you are asked to **explain** something, it is not enough just to state or describe it.

Your answer must contain some reasoning or justification of the points you make.

Your explanation can include mathematical explanations, if calculations are needed.

The term efficiency is explained, an equation for calculating the efficiency is provided and a value is calculated for the fan's efficiency.

The question expects you to talk about **energy stores** and **energy transfers**. There are eight types of energy store and four types of energy transfer, which you can read more about on page 15.

Now try this

Describe an experiment to determine how powerful three weightlifters are.

Your answer should refer to the equations for calculating changes in gravitational potential energy and power.

(6 marks)

Interacting forces

Pairs of forces can interact **at a distance** or by **direct contact**.

Non-contact forces

Forces can be exerted between objects without them being in contact with one another. There are three **non-contact forces** that you need to know about.

Gravity acts between all masses. It is always attractive.

Magnetism acts between magnetic poles. Unlike poles attract and like poles repel.

Electrostatic charges exert forces on each other at a distance. Unlike charges attract and like charges repel.

Contact forces

Forces can be exerted between objects due to them being in contact. In each case there is an interaction pair of forces that act in opposite directions. The forces can be represented by vectors.

The **normal contact force** acts upwards in opposition to the weight of the object. The interaction pair is the force of the ground on the box and the force of the box on the ground.

The **force of friction** acts in opposition to the pushing force that is trying to change its motion. Friction always acts to slow a moving object down. The interaction pair is the force of the object on the surface and the force of the surface on the object.

Worked example

An archer fires an arrow from a bow. Describe the contact and non-contact forces involved in firing the arrow. **(2 marks)**

Contact forces include the normal force acting on the arrow, friction as it moves through the air and the tension in the string. Non-contact forces include gravity once it has been released.

Other examples of contact forces include tension, upthrust and drag.

Now try this

1. State how gravity is different from magnetism and the electrostatic force. **(1 mark)**

2. State how the forces of friction and drag are similar. **(1 mark)**

3. Describe the contact and non-contact forces acting on a moving ship. **(3 marks)**

Moments

Forces which act at a **distance** from a **pivot** can cause a **turning effect** or rotation. This is known as a **moment**.

Moments

The size of the moment, or turning effect, is given by the equation:

moment (newton-metres, Nm) = force (N) × distance normal to the direction of the force (m)

LEARN IT!
IT'S NOT ON THE EQUATIONS LIST

The distance must be measured from the pivot normal (at right angles, or **perpendicular**) to the direction of the force. The pivot is the point about which the object rotates.

nut
spanner
force
distance to pivot

Worked example

Two children are sitting on a seesaw.
(a) Calculate the anticlockwise moment.

(2 marks)

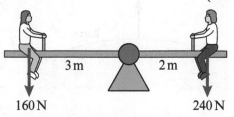

3 m   2 m
160 N   240 N

= 160 N × 3 m = 480 Nm

(b) Calculate the clockwise moment.   **(2 marks)**

= 240 N × 2 m = 480 Nm

(c) Explain why the seesaw doesn't move.

(2 marks)

The anticlockwise and clockwise moments about the pivot are equal so the seesaw is balanced and does not move.

The principle of moments

LEARN IT!
IT'S NOT ON THE EQUATIONS LIST

pivot
beam
0.3 m   0.1 m
20 N
W N

sum of the clockwise moments = sum of the anticlockwise moments

for rotational forces in equilibrium.

The diagram shows a common arrangement for weighing fruit and vegetables, as well as babies. The beam is balanced so:

anticlockwise moment = clockwise moment

20 N × 0.3 m = W N × 0.1 m

W = 6 Nm/0.1 m = 60 N

The weight of the bar has been ignored in this calculation.

Worked example

A uniform wooden beam of length 3 m is pivoted at its centre. Calculate the weight that needs to be placed at point X for the beam to balance.   **(4 marks)**

X N   20 N
1.2 m   1.5 m

When the beam is balanced it is in equilibrium.

Sum of clockwise moments = sum of anticlockwise moments

or $F_1 × d_1 = F_2 × d_2$

20 N × 1.5 m = X N × 1.2 m or 30 Nm = 1.2 m × X N

so X = 30 Nm ÷ 1.2 m = 25 N

Now try this

1 A force of 25 N acts at a distance of 2 m from a pivot. Calculate the size of the moment.

(3 marks)

2 A uniform wooden beam of length 3 m is pivoted at its centre. A weight of 30 N is placed 1 m away from the pivot on the left. Calculate the size of the weight that would need to be placed at a distance of 1.5 m to the right of the pivot for the beam to balance.   **(4 marks)**

Levers and gears

Levers and **gears** can transmit the **rotational effect** of forces.

Levers

A **lever** can be used to cause rotation. The nature of this rotation depends on the position of:

1 the **input force** – the force provided by the user of the lever

2 the **output force** – the force that results from the input force

3 the **fulcrum** – the turning point about which both forces act.

For different levers, the input force, output force and fulcrum are in different positions relative to each other.

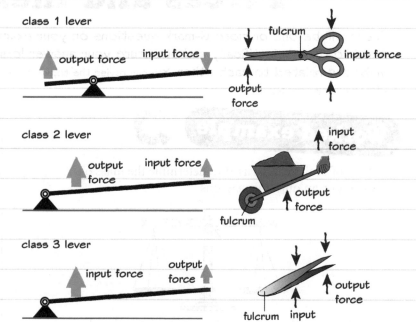

class 1 lever

class 2 lever

class 3 lever

Gears

Gears are toothed wheels that are meshed together to transmit rotational force and motion. This is a low gear.

Each gear in a series reverses the direction of motion.

input

output

A larger gear will rotate more slowly than a smaller gear, but will have a greater turning effect. A low gear leads to a low speed and a high turning effect.

High gears and low gears

A high gear is when a large input gear turns a smaller output gear. This leads to a **high speed** and a **low turning effect**.

A low gear is when a smaller input gear turns a larger output gear. This leads to a **low speed** and a **high turning effect**.

Worked example

Describe the common features of gears and levers in terms of how they work.

(2 marks)

Gear and levers both transmit the rotational effect of a force and they can alter the size of the output force compared with the input force.

You need to know that both gears and levers can cause rotation and can alter the size of the output force.

Now try this

Look at page 68 on moments. Consider the turning moment and describe how this affects the relative sizes of the forces.

1 Give one example of an
  (a) class 1 lever **(1 mark)**
  (b) class 2 lever **(1 mark)**
  (c) class 3 lever. **(1 mark)**

2 Describe the speed and turning effect for
  (a) a high gear **(2 marks)**
  (b) a low gear. **(2 marks)**

3 Describe how levers and gears can cause rotation to happen. **(4 marks)**

Extended response – Forces and their effects

There will be one or more 6-mark questions on your exam paper. For these questions, you will need to think scientifically and structure your answer logically, showing how the points you make are related to each other. You can revise the topics for this question, which is about **forces and their effects**, on pages 67–69.

Worked example

A set of scales can be used to determine the mass or weight of an object in newtons.

Explain how the scales can be used to determine the weight of an object that is placed on the plate below point X.

Your answer should refer to the forces involved and the principle of moments. **(6 marks)**

When a mass is placed on plate X, there will be a force acting downwards due to the gravitational force acting on the mass. This force will lead to a clockwise moment that is equal to the size of the force X perpendicular distance of the force at X from point Z.

To determine the weight of the object at X, weights are now added to the plate below W until it becomes horizontal. When this happens the clockwise moment and the anticlockwise moment must be the same, so the scales are balanced or in equilibrium.

If the distance from W to Z is the same as the distance from X to Z, the total weight of the weights on plate W must be the same as the weight of the object on plate X.

Command word: Explain

When you are asked to explain something, it is not enough to just state or describe something. Your answer must contain some reasoning or justification of the points you make based on the appropriate physics. This needs to be communicated clearly using good spelling, punctuation and grammar.

> The nature of the force and the size and direction of the moment at point X are addressed here.

> An explanation of what needs to happen to bring the scales back into equilibrium is given here, as well as the nature and direction of any forces or moments acting at plate W.

> An explanation of how the weight of the body on plate X can be determined from the weight at point W is provided here.

It is important to remember that the principle of moments only applies to bodies that are in equilibrium, where there is no overall rotation. Only when the scales are in equilibrium can the unknown force or weight be determined. It is also important not to confuse weight and mass. Mass is a measure of matter in a body and is measured in kilograms (kg), whereas weight is the force of gravity acting downwards on a body and is measured in newtons (N). To convert from a force or weight to a mass, you need to divide by the gravitational field strength, g, which is approximately 10 N/kg.

Now try this

Describe what can happen when two objects interact with one another. Your answer should refer to contact and non-contact forces. **(6 marks)**

Circuit symbols

Electric circuit diagrams are drawn using agreed symbols and conventions that can be understood by everybody across the world.

Circuit symbols

You need to know the symbols for these components.

Component	Symbol	Purpose
cell (battery)	positive terminal ⊣⊢ negative terminal	provides a potential difference
switches		allows the current flow to be switched on or off
voltmeter	–(V)–	measures potential difference across a component
ammeter	–(A)–	measures the current flowing through a component
fixed resistor	–▭–	provides a fixed resistance to the flow of current
variable resistor		provides a variable (changeable) resistance
filament lamp	–⊗–	converts electrical energy to light energy as a useful form
motor	–(M)–	converts electrical energy to kinetic energy as a useful form
diode	–▷|–	allows current to flow in one direction only
thermistor		resistance decreases when the temperature increases
LDR		resistance decreases when the light intensity increases
LED		a diode that gives out light when current flows through it

Worked example

Name four components that are commonly used to change or control the amount of resistance in a circuit. **(2 marks)**

thermistor, LDR, fixed resistor, variable resistor

2 marks for all correct, 1 mark for 3 correct and zero marks for less than 3 correct.

Worked example

Describe how an LED is different from a filament lamp. **(1 mark)**

An LED will only allow electrical current to pass through it in one direction.

Now try this

1 State which components above are output devices. **(3 marks)**

2 State how ammeters and voltmeters should be arranged with components in circuits. **(2 marks)**
3 Design a circuit to turn on a lamp when it goes dark. **(3 marks)**

Series and parallel circuits

Components in circuits can be arranged in **series** or **parallel**. The rules for current and potential difference in these two types of circuits are different.

Series circuits

A **series circuit** contains just one loop, around which an electric current can flow.

Electrons do not flow through any of the voltmeters.

Electrons flow clockwise in this circuit, through the cell, wires, three ammeters and two resistors.

Ammeters are always connected in series with components.

Ammeters have a very low resistance so the current can flow through them and be measured accurately.

The size of the current in a series circuit is the same at every point in the circuit. All three ammeters in this circuit will show the same value for the current.

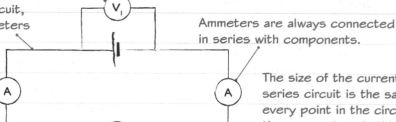

The potential difference across components that are arranged in series must add up to give the cell voltage, so $V_1 = V_2 + V_3$.

Voltmeters have a very high resistance so that no current will flow through them.

Parallel circuits

A **parallel circuit** contains more than one loop and the current will split up or recombine at the junctions.

The potential difference across the components in each branch of a parallel circuit must add to give the cell voltage. The voltmeter readings across the two resistors will both have the same value as the potential difference across the cell.

The sum of the currents in each of the branches must equal the current leaving the cell. For this example,
$A_1 = A_4 = A_2 + A_3$.

 Worked example

What are the missing values in this parallel circuit if the bulbs are identical?   **(2 marks)**

Both the ammeter readings A_3 and $A_4 = 1$ A. The voltmeter readings V_3 and V_4 will both be 6 V.

 Now try this

1 Describe the differences for current and potential difference in series and parallel circuits.   **(4 marks)**

2 Explain why car lights are connected in parallel and not in series.   **(3 marks)**

3 Explain why a cell goes flat more quickly when lamps are arranged in parallel.   **(4 marks)**

4 The bulbs in this circuit are identical. What are the missing values in this series circuit for A_1, A_2, V_1 and V_2?   **(2 marks)**

Current and charge

An **electric current** is the **rate of flow of charge**. In a metal, electric current is the flow of electrons.

Charge and current

The size of a current is a measure of how much charge flows past a point each second. It is the rate of flow of charge. The unit of charge is the **coulomb** (C). One ampere, or amp (A), is one coulomb of charge per second. You can calculate charge using the equation:

Charge (C) = current (A) × time (s)

$$Q = I \times t$$

LEARN IT!
IT'S NOT ON THE EQUATIONS LIST

Watch out! Don't get the units and quantities confused. The units have sensible abbreviations (C for coulombs, A for amps). The symbols for the quantities are not as easy to remember (Q stands for charge, I for current).

You also need to know how to rearrange the equation using the triangle shown so that you can calculate Q, I and t using values provided in questions.

Measuring current

Electric current will flow in a closed circuit when there is a source of potential difference. To measure the size of the current flowing through a component, an ammeter is connected in series with the component.

Conventional current flows this way, from + to − in a circuit.

The current flowing is the same at all points in a series circuit. In this example, the current is 0.5 A.

The cell is the source of potential difference.

Electrons flow this way, from − to +.

The three ammeters are connected in series with the two filament lamps.

Worked example

(a) Describe how ammeters should be connected with components in circuits. **(1 mark)**

Ammeters should always be arranged in series with the component to be measured.

(b) Describe what happens to the size of the current in a series circuit. **(1 mark)**

The current is the same value at any point in a series circuit.

Worked example

(a) A current of 1.5 A flows for 2 minutes. Calculate how much charge flows in this time. **(3 marks)**

$Q = I \times t$

   $= 1.5 A \times 120 s = 180 C$

(b) A charge of 1200 C flows through a filament lamp for 4 minutes. Calculate the average current in the filament lamp. **(3 marks)**

$I = Q \div t$

   $= 1200 C \div 240 s = 5 A$

Now try this

There are 60 × 60 seconds in one hour.

1 State the units of current and charge. **(2 marks)**

2 Calculate the charge that flows in one hour when there is a current of 0.25 A in a circuit. **(3 marks)**

3 A charge of 3000 C is transferred by a current of 0.25 A. Calculate the length of time for which the current flows. **(4 marks)**

Energy and charge

Energy, **charge** and **potential difference** are closely related when dealing with electrical circuits.

Energy, charge and potential difference

Energy, charge and potential difference are related by the equation:

energy transferred (J) = charge moved (C) × potential difference (V)

$$E = Q \times V$$

LEARN IT!
IT'S NOT ON THE EQUATIONS LIST

Calculate the charge, Q, from the current reading on the ammeter using the equation $Q = I \times t$ (see page 73).

Maths skills Cover up the quantity you want to find with your finger. The position of the other two quantities tells you the formula.

Triangle: E over $Q \times V$

Remember that for this circuit, the value obtained for the energy transferred will be for this bulb, since the potential difference being measured is across this bulb only.

The potential difference, V, across the bulb is measured with a voltmeter. Voltmeters are always connected in parallel with components and ammeters are always connected in series.

Worked example

(a) A charge of 25 C passes through a motor. The potential difference across the motor is 6 V. Calculate how much energy is transferred. **(3 marks)**

$E = Q \times V$, so $E = 25C \times 6V = 150J$

For some calculations, you just need to substitute the numbers straight into the equation $E = Q \times V$.

(b) A current of 1.2 A flows through a bulb for 2 minutes. The potential difference across the bulb is 12 V. Work out how much energy is transferred. **(3 marks)**

$E = Q \times V$ and $Q = I \times t$, so $E = I \times t \times V$

$E = 1.2A \times 120s \times 12V = 1728J$

For other calculations, there may be two steps. Here you need to calculate Q first by using $Q = I \times t$ and then substitute this value into $E = Q \times V$.

Worked example

A charge of 18 C transfers 364 J of electrical energy through a resistor. Calculate the potential difference across the resistor. **(3 marks)**

Rearrange $E = Q \times V$ to give $V = E \div Q$.

$V = 364J \div 18C = 20.2V$

Now try this

1 A charge of 24 C flows through an LED and the potential difference across it is 6 V. Calculate how much energy is transferred. **(3 marks)**

2 Explain why the volt, V, can also be described as a 'joule per coulomb'. **(3 marks)**

3 400 J of energy are transferred through a lamp by 50 C of electric charge. Calculate the potential difference across the lamp. **(4 marks)**

Ohm's law

Ohm's law states how the **current** through a component relates to its **resistance** and the **potential difference** across it.

Resistance

The **resistance** of a component is a way of measuring how hard it is for electricity to flow through it. The units for resistance are **ohms (Ω)**.

The resistance of a whole circuit depends on the resistances of the different components in the circuit. The higher the total resistance, the smaller the current.

resistance UP, current DOWN

The resistance of a circuit can be changed by putting different **resistors** into the circuit, or by using a **variable resistor**. The resistance of a variable resistor can be changed using a slider or knob.

Ohm's law

Ohm's law states that the size of the current, *I*, flowing through a component of resistance, *R*, is directly proportional to the potential difference, *V*, across the component at constant temperature.

The equation for Ohm's law is:

potential difference (V) = current (A) × resistance (Ω)

$$V = I \times R$$

LEARN IT!
IT'S NOT ON THE EQUATIONS LIST

Components that obey Ohm's law are said to be ohmic conductors whereas those that do not obey Ohm's law are non-ohmic. Examples of both of these can be found on page 77.

Worked example

(a) Resistor A has a current of 3 A flowing through it when the potential difference across it is 15 V. What is the size of its resistance? **(3 marks)**

From $V = I \times R$ you obtain $R = V / I$

Substituting gives $R = 15 \text{V} / 3 \text{A} = 5 \Omega$

(b) Sketch a circuit that could be used to plot current against potential difference for this resistor. **(4 marks)**

The variable resistor can be used to collect numerous values for *I* and *V* so that an I–V graph can be plotted.

(c) Resistor A is then replaced with resistor B. A graph of current against potential difference is plotted.

Explain what the graph tells you about the two resistors. **(2 marks)**

The steeper line shows that resistor A has a lower resistance than resistor B.

Both resistors are ohmic because the graphs are straight lines.

Now try this

1 A current of 3.2 A flows through a lamp of resistance 18 Ω. Calculate the size of the potential difference across the lamp. **(3 marks)**

2 The potential difference across a resistor is 28 V when the current flowing through it is 0.4 A. Calculate the resistance of the resistor. **(3 marks)**

Resistors

The arrangement of resistors in **series** or **parallel** determines whether the **resistance** in a circuit **increases** or **decreases**.

Resistors in series

Calculating series resistance

For resistors arranged in series:

1 The current through each resistor is the same value.

2 The sum of the voltages across the resistors must add up to equal the cell voltage.

The total resistance in this series circuit is $12\,\Omega$. The total potential difference from the battery is $6\,V$. Using $I = V \div R$ the current, I, flowing in resistors P and Q, is $6\,V \div 12\,\Omega = 0.5\,A$.

Resistors in parallel

Calculating parallel resistance

For resistors arranged in parallel:

1 The total current leaving the battery is equal to the sum of the current flowing in the separate branches.

2 The potential difference across the resistors in each branch is equal to the potential difference of the battery.

Worked example

In the series circuit in the diagram, resistor X is known to have a resistance of $16\,\Omega$.

(a) Calculate the missing potential difference value across resistor Y. **(2 marks)**

8 V, since the values across X and Y must add up to 12 V.

(b) Calculate the current flowing through resistor X. **(3 marks)**

$I = V \div R = 4\,V \div 16\,\Omega = 0.25\,A$

Worked example

Two resistors are arranged in parallel as shown in the circuit below. Calculate:

(a) the resistance of Y **(2 marks)**

$R = V \div I = 12\,V \div 0.3\,A = 40\,\Omega$

(b) the current through resistor X **(2 marks)**

$I = V \div R = 12\,V \div 20\,\Omega = 0.6\,A$

(c) the total current supplied by the battery. **(2 marks)**

total current = $0.3\,A + 0.6\,A = 0.9\,A$

Now try this

Two resistors, each of resistance 60 ohms, are arranged in series and connected to a 12 V cell. Calculate the size of the current flowing in the circuit. **(3 marks)**

I–V graphs

An **I–V graph** shows how the **current** flowing through a component varies as the **potential difference** across it varies. You need to know the characteristics of these I–V graphs.

① Fixed resistor   **② Filament lamp**   **③ Diode**

The temperature remains constant so the resistance remains constant. The slope or gradient is constant and the line remains straight throughout.

As the potential difference increases, the filament gets hotter, and atomic vibration increases. This leads to greater resistance. The slope or gradient decreases as the potential difference increases since resistance is increasing.

The current only flows in one direction. There is a **threshold** in the forward direction, which is why the graph is flat initially. A diode behaves like a fixed resistor – the resistance does not change. A diode has a very high resistance in the reverse direction.

Drawing an I–V graph

You can use a circuit like this to collect data about current and potential difference.

✓ When the switch is closed you can read current from the ammeter and potential difference from the voltmeter.

✓ Varying the value of the variable resistor allows you to record the current for different potential differences.

✓ You can reverse the cell to obtain negative values for potential difference.

Component to be tested is placed here

Worked example

A student is testing the resistance of a component. She draws an I–V graph.

The component being tested is a
☐ **A** diode
☐ **B** filament lamp
☒ **C** fixed resistor
☐ **D** cell   **(1 mark)**

An I–V graph always has the current (I) plotted on the vertical y-axis and the potential difference (V) plotted on the horizontal x-axis. To find the resistance of a component from an I–V graph, you will need to divide the x-axis value by the corresponding y-axis value. That is, the gradient is not the resistance, the gradient = 1/resistance.

Now try this

Amy is testing the resistance of a filament lamp. She varies the potential difference across the lamp and records the current that flows.

(a) Sketch a graph of potential difference (V) against current (I) for Amy's experiment.
                                              (2 marks)

(b) Explain the shape of your graph.   **(3 marks)**

Electrical circuits

Practical skills You can investigate the relationship between **potential difference**, **current** and **resistance** for a filament lamp and a resistor by arranging them in series and parallel circuits.

Core practical

Aim

To determine the relationship between potential difference, current and resistance for a filament lamp and a resistor when arranged in series and parallel.

Apparatus

cell or battery, ammeters, voltmeters, filament lamps, resistors, connecting wires

Method 1: Investigating V, I and R

Set up the circuit so that the current through the filament lamp and the potential difference across it can be measured. Adjust the variable resistor setting to obtain a number of readings for current and potential difference. Plot a graph of I against V. Repeat for the resistor.

Results

Your results can be recorded in a table.

Potential difference (V)	Current (I)
−2.0	−0.20
−1.5	−0.18
−1.0	−0.15
−0.5	−0.10
0	0
0.5	0.10
1.0	0.16
1.5	0.18
2.0	0.20

Method 2: Testing series and parallel circuits

Set up the circuits in both parallel and series arrangements and use these to verify the rules for the behaviour of current and potential difference in both types of circuits.

There is more information relating to current, potential difference, resistance and series and parallel circuits on pages 72–77.

Be careful when using electrical circuits as electric current can produce heat and cause burns.

Data collected in an investigation are accurate if close to the true value. The data are precise if the repeat readings of a certain variable are close to one another. The best data is both accurate and precise.

In order to improve the accuracy of your results, place a switch in your circuit so that the current does not get too large. Too large a current leads to a greater value of the resistance being recorded, due to thermal energy causing extra vibrations of the ions in the metal lattice.

Now try this

1 Explain why a series or parallel arrangement will still lead to the same shape of I–V graph for both components. **(4 marks)**
2 Explain why the I–V graph for a filament lamp has the shape that it does. **(5 marks)**

Conclusion

Current is the same at any point in a series circuit, but will split up at a junction in a parallel circuit.

The sum of the potential difference across components in any loop in a series or parallel circuit equals the potential difference of the cell.

The LDR and the thermistor

The resistance of **light-dependent resistors (LDRs)** and **thermistors** changes according to light conditions (LDR) or temperature (thermistor).

Light-dependent resistors

The resistance of a **light-dependent resistor (LDR)** is large in the dark. The resistance gets less if light shines on it. The brighter the light, the lower the resistance.

brightness **UP**, resistance **DOWN**

Thermistors

The resistance of a **thermistor** depends on its temperature. The higher the temperature, the lower the resistance.

temperature **UP**, resistance **DOWN**

Worked example

A 6 V battery is connected in series with an LDR, a 300 Ω fixed resistor and an ammeter, as shown.

(a) Describe how the circuit shown can be used to explore the variation in resistance as the light levels change. **(2 marks)**

The amount of light being shone on the LDR can be changed by varying the intensity of the light it is exposed to from a torch or a lamp. The size of the current flowing in the circuit can then be recorded for each of these light levels.

(b) Describe the results you would expect. **(2 marks)**

The output current will be highest when the light level is greatest. As the brightness increases, the LDR's resistance decreases.

(c) How could a voltmeter be used in the circuit to show how the resistance changes with light levels? **(3 marks)**

Connect a voltmeter across the LDR. As the light level increases, the potential difference across the LDR will decrease since the resistance has decreased and a greater share of the 6 V will be across the fixed resistor.

Worked example

A 3 V battery is connected in series with a thermistor, as shown.

(a) Explain how the circuit can be used to explore how the resistance of the thermistor changes. **(2 marks)**

The thermistor could be immersed in a beaker of cold water, or a water bath, which is then heated from 10 °C to 80 °C. The current flowing in the circuit is recorded at each temperature over this range.

(b) Describe what your results would show. **(2 marks)**

As the temperature increases, the current increases. This is because the thermistor's resistance decreases as it gets warmer.

If a buzzer was placed in this circuit then it could be used as a simple fire alarm, with the buzzer sounding when the current reached a certain value. This could be controlled or calibrated by using a variable resistor.

Now try this

1 State what affects the resistance of (a) a thermistor and (b) an LDR. **(2 marks)**

2 Describe how an LDR and a thermistor could be used together in a circuit. **(4 marks)**

Current heating effect

When a **current** flows in a circuit it has a **heating** effect. This can have **advantages** and **disadvantages**.

Energy transfers in a resistor

When there is an electric current flowing through a resistor, energy is transferred which heats the resistor.

Electrical energy is **dissipated** as thermal energy in the surroundings when an electrical current does work against electrical resistance.

Unwanted thermal energy transfers can be reduced by using low-resistance wires. Wires that are better conductors, shorter or thicker will waste less energy as heat compared with longer, thinner wires of a poorer electrical conductor.

Energy and collisions

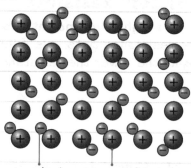

electrons   metal ions

Electrons flow through a metal lattice when a potential difference is applied across the ends of the metal. Collisions between the electrons and the ions in the lattice lead to the kinetic energy of the electrons being dissipated as thermal energy.

Advantages of the heating effect

Some appliances such as the iron, the heater and the fuse are designed to transfer energy to thermal energy by the heating effect of a current.

The heating effect of a current passing through a resistor is useful for:
- heating water in a kettle
- radiant heaters
- toasters, grills and ovens
- underfloor heating.

Disadvantages of the heating effect

If too much current flows in a circuit, then the heating effect can lead to the appliance catching fire or the user becoming burned.

Too much current can flow if too many appliances are being used at the same time. Safety features such as correct fuses, circuit breakers and earthing need to be in place. See page 83.

In many devices, the heating effect of a current means that some energy is wasted. For example, a light bulb and a TV screen transfer some energy to thermal energy by the heating effect of a current.

Worked example

Give three examples of appliances in the home where the heating effect of the current causes energy to be wasted as thermal energy.

(1 mark)

a computer, computer monitor and a mobile phone screen

Worked example

Explain how energy is transferred to thermal energy in a resistor. **(3 marks)**

Collisions between the moving electrons and the fixed metal ions in a lattice result in the kinetic energy of the electrons being transferred to thermal energy. The thermal energy is dissipated into the surroundings.

Now try this

 1 Name three household devices that usefully transfer electrical energy to thermal energy.
(3 marks)

 2 Explain why it might be dangerous to have many electrical appliances being used at the same time. **(3 marks)**

 3 Explain how electrical energy is dissipated as thermal energy when a potential difference is applied across the ends of a metal wire.
(4 marks)

Dissipated means energy lost to surroundings.

Energy and power

Electrical energy is **transferred** in circuits to do **work**. The amount of energy transferred depends on the **current, time** and **potential difference**.

Calculating energy

The total energy transferred by a device depends on the current in it, the potential difference across it and how long it is switched on.

$$\text{Energy transferred (J)} = \text{current (A)} \times \text{potential difference (V)} \times \text{time (s)}$$

$$E = I \times V \times t$$

Maths skills Cover up the quantity you want to find with your finger. The position of the other quantities tells you the formula.

$$V = E \div (I \times t)$$
$$I = E \div (V \times t)$$
$$t = E \div (V \times I)$$

Calculating power

Power is the energy transferred per second or the rate at which energy is transferred. It is measured in **watts**. For electrical devices, power depends on the current in the device and the potential difference across it, or the resistance of the device. It also depends on the total energy transferred and the time taken to transfer the energy.

Maths skills The equation triangles for power can be used in the same way as for energy calculations.

There are three equations you need to know that can be used to calculate power:

1 electrical power (W) = current (A) × potential difference (V)
$$P = I \times V$$

LEARN IT! IT'S NOT ON THE EQUATIONS LIST

2 power (W) = energy transferred (J) ÷ time taken (s)
$$P = E \div t$$

LEARN IT! IT'S NOT ON THE EQUATIONS LIST

3 electrical power (W) = current squared (A²) × resistance (Ω)
$$P = I^2 \times R$$

LEARN IT! IT'S NOT ON THE EQUATIONS LIST

Worked example

(a) A current of 8 A flows for 4 minutes in a kettle that is connected to a potential difference of 230 V. Calculate how much energy is transferred. **(4 marks)**

$E = V \times I \times t$

$E = 230\,V \times 8\,A \times (4 \times 60)\,s = 441\,600\,J$

(b) A 2.2 kW hairdryer is used for 5 minutes. Calculate how much energy is transferred. **(4 marks)**

$E = P \times t$

$= 2200\,W \times (5 \times 60)\,s = 660\,000\,J$

Worked example

(a) Calculate the power of a microwave that transfers 30 000 J of energy in 35 s. **(4 marks)**

$P = E \div t$

$= 30\,000\,J \div 35\,s = 857\,W$

(b) Calculate the current that is taken by a device with a power rating of 3400 W when its resistance is 120 Ω. **(4 marks)**

$I = \sqrt{(P \div R)} = \sqrt{(3400\,W \div 120\,\Omega)} = 5.3\,A$

Power can be measured in watts (W) or in joules per second (J/s). A power of 1 W means that 1 J of energy is being transferred each second.

Now try this

1 Calculate the power of an electric oven when 13 A flows through it when it is connected to the 230 V mains supply. **(3 marks)**

2 A current of 1.5 A flows for 2 minutes when a potential difference of 12 V is applied across the ends of a resistor. Calculate the amount of energy that is transferred. **(3 marks)**

A.c. and d.c. circuits

Circuits can be operated using **alternating current (a.c.)** or **direct current (d.c.)**.

Direct current

An **electric current** in a wire is a flow of electrons. The current supplied by **cells** and **batteries** is **direct current (d.c.)**. In a direct current the electrons all flow in the same direction.

cell

Electrons are pushed out of one end of the cell.

Electrons flow round to the other end of the cell.

There must be a complete circuit for the electrons to flow.

The oscilloscope trace for d.c. from a battery is a horizontal line. The potential difference can be read off the vertical scale.

The potential difference above has a constant value of 2.8 V.

Alternating current

Mains electricity supplied to homes and businesses is an **alternating current (a.c.)**. Alternating current is an electric current that changes direction regularly, and its potential difference is constantly changing.

For an a.c. supply, the movement of charge is constantly changing direction. The mains supply has an average working value of 230 V and a frequency of 50 Hz. This means that the electric current and voltage change direction 100 times every second.

D.c. and a.c. supply in the home

Both d.c. and a.c. can be used in the home. D.c. is supplied in the form of cells and batteries. A.c. is the mains supply. Both can be used by devices to transfer energy to motors and heating devices.

Different electrical appliances have different power ratings. The power rating tells you how much energy is transferred by the appliance each second.

Appliance	Power rating
kettle	2200 W
hairdryer	1500 W
microwave	850 W
electric oven	3000 W
electric shaver	15 W

Worked example

Compare the power rating of a hairdryer and an electric shaver, and the changes in stored energy when they are in use. **(4 marks)**

The hairdryer has a power rating of 1500 W, which means that it transfers 1500 J per second to stores of kinetic energy and thermal energy. The electric shaver has a power rating of one-hundredth of the hair dryer. It transfers only 15 J per second, mainly to a kinetic energy store.

Now try this

1 Give three examples of devices that use
   (a) d.c. **(3 marks)**
   (b) a.c. **(3 marks)**
2 Explain how a.c. and d.c. are
   (a) similar **(1 mark)**
   (b) different. **(2 marks)**
3 A 15 W electric shaver and a 3000 W electric oven are both used for the same amount of time. Compare the amount of energy transferred for the two appliances.
   (3 marks)

Mains electricity and the plug

Electrical energy enters UK homes as **mains electricity** at **230V a.c.** A mains plug has three wires, which have different roles in the operation of a.c. in the home.

The 13A plug

The earth (yellow and green) wire does not form part of the circuit but acts as a safety feature along with the fuse.

The neutral (blue) wire completes the circuit with the appliance. It is at a potential difference of 0V with respect to the earth wire.

The live, neutral and earth wires are made from copper, but covered in colour-coded insulating plastic so that the consumer is not exposed to a dangerous voltage.

The live (brown) wire carries the supply to the appliance. It is at a potential difference of 230V with respect to the neutral and earth wires.

The fuse is connected to the live wire and it contains a wire that will melt if the current gets too high. If the fuse blows, the device will be at 0V and not at 230V. A switch should also be connected in the live wire for the same reason.

Earthing and fuses

Earthing, circuit breakers and fuses are safety features that are used to ensure that the user does not get electrocuted if a fault occurs.

1. The live wire inside the appliance may come loose and touch a metal part of the device's casing.

2. The large current heats and melts the wire in the fuse, making a break in the circuit.

5. By having an earth wire connected to the metal casing, the user is not at risk if the live wire comes loose and touches anything metallic.

3. The earth wire is connected to the metal casing and a large current flows in through the live wire and out through the earth wire.

4. The circuit is no longer complete, so there is no chance of electric shock or fire.

Worked example

(a) State the potential differences of the live, neutral and earth wires in a plug. **(3 marks)**

live: 230V; neutral and earth: both at 0V

(b) Name three safety features used by appliances. **(3 marks)**

earth wire, fuse and circuit breaker

Circuit breakers are also used as safety features in addition to fuses and earth wires. When circuit breakers detect that a current is too high, they use a magnetic field to open a switch and isolate the appliance, making it safe. They are easily reset by pressing a switch if they trip.

Now try this

1 State the colours of the
  (a) live wire **(1 mark)**
  (b) neutral wire **(1 mark)**
  (c) earth wire. **(1 mark)**

2 Give one advantage of a fuse and one advantage of a circuit breaker. **(2 marks)**

3 Explain how an earth wire and fuse protect the user when the live wire comes loose. **(4 marks)**

Extended response – Electricity and circuits

There will be one or more 6-mark questions on your exam paper. For these questions, you will need to think scientifically and structure your answer logically, showing how the points you make are related to each other. You can revise the topics for this question, which is about **electricity and circuits**, on pages 33 and 71–83.

Worked example

Two identical bulbs can be connected to a 6 V cell in series or parallel as shown in the diagram.

Compare the brightness of the bulbs in the two circuits when the switches are closed.

Your answer should refer to the current, potential difference, energy stores and rates of energy transfer in both circuits.

(6 marks)

The brightness of the bulbs in the series circuit will be much less than the brightness of the bulbs in the parallel circuit.

The electrical energy that is transferred to light is directly proportional to the potential difference across each bulb and the size of the current flowing through each bulb. The brightness of the bulbs will be greatest when the energy transferred per second is greatest.

In the series circuit, the potential difference across each bulb will be 3 V, whereas in the parallel circuit the potential difference across each bulb will be 6 V. Also, the current flowing through each of the bulbs in the parallel circuit will be greater than the current flowing through the bulbs in the series circuit. Since the current and the potential difference in the parallel bulbs are greater, more energy will be transferred per second and the bulb will be brighter.

 The opening sentence simply states how the brightness of the lamps compares in each of the two circuits.

 The answer then states the relationship between electrical energy, current and potential difference before relating brightness to the energy transferred per second, or power, of the bulbs.

The comparison of the bulbs' brightness is related to the relative sizes of any current, potential difference and energy transferred per second.

 The rate at which energy is transferred from one form to another is called power. When dealing with electrical circuits, the power is calculated using the equation $P = IV$. You can read more about this on page 81.

Now try this

The UK mains electricity supply operates at 230 V a.c. Explain how safety features help to keep users safe. Your answer should refer to the structure and function of a plug. **(6 marks)**

Static electricity

Static electricity occurs when electric charges are transferred **onto**, or **off**, the surface of an **insulator**. This causes the insulator to gain a **positive** or a **negative** charge.

Negatively charged insulators

Insulators become **negatively charged** when **electrons** move **onto** the **insulator** from the cloth due to **friction**.

polythene rod

Negative rod, positive cloth

When **polythene** is rubbed with a cloth, electrons are transferred by **friction** from the **cloth** to the **rod**. Since electrons are **negatively** charged, the rod becomes **negatively charged** and the cloth becomes **positively charged**. These charges are **equal** and **opposite**.

It is **always** the **electron** that is transferred when insulators become charged by friction.

Positively charged insulators

Insulators become positively charged when electrons move **off** the **insulator** and onto the cloth due to the force of **friction**.

Positive rod, **negative** cloth

When **acetate** is rubbed with a cloth, electrons are transferred by **friction** from the **rod** to the **cloth**. Again, since electrons are negatively charged, the **cloth** becomes **negatively charged** and the **acetate rod** becomes **positively charged**. Again, these charges will be **equal** and **opposite**.

Worked example

Describe what happens when two electrically charged objects are brought close together.

(3 marks)

The charged objects exert a force on each other. If the two objects have the same type of electrical charge they repel each other. If they have different types of electrical charge they attract each other.

Now try this

1 What charge will an insulator have if it
   (a) gains electrons   **(1 mark)**
   (b) loses electrons?   **(1 mark)**
2 Which objects will attract each other?
   ☐ **A** two negatively charged rods
   ☐ **B** a positively charged duster and a negatively charged rod
   ☐ **C** two positively charged objects
   ☐ **D** a neutral rod and a neutral duster   **(1 mark)**

3 Explain why insulators never become charged by gaining or losing protons.   **(3 marks)**
4 Polythene gains electrons when rubbed. Explain how you could use a polythene rod to tell if an insulator were positively charged.   **(3 marks)**

Electrostatic phenomena

Electrostatic behaviour can be seen in action every day.

Electric shocks

Electrons can be transferred onto your clothes by friction. They stay on your clothes because the materials from which clothes are made are insulators. However, if you then touch a metal handle, the electrons can conduct to earth and you will receive an electric shock. This is an example of earthing.

Lightning strikes

Lightning occurs because of electrostatic induction:

1. Ice particles in clouds gain electrons from other ice particles by friction as they rub against each other.

2. The bottom of the cloud gains electrons and a negative charge.

3. Electrons in the ground are repelled by the bottom of the cloud.

4. Lightning jumps to earth as a spark of electrons.

Electrostatic induction

A **charged object** (such as a plastic comb) can attract **uncharged objects** (such as small pieces of paper). This happens because the comb **induces** a charge in the pieces of paper.

Electrostatic induction involves an opposite charge being induced on the surface of a neutral insulator by another charged insulator. In both cases, the force of attraction is seen.

The balloon has a negative charge.

The electrons in the wall are repelled and move away.

The positive charge left behind (the **induced charge**) attracts the negative charge on the balloon.

Worked example

Explain how small pieces of paper are attracted by electrostatic induction by a comb when the comb is rubbed with a cloth. **(4 marks)**

Friction occurs between the cloth and the comb.

Electrons are transferred between these insulators so that one becomes positive and the other one negative.

When the comb is placed near the paper, the opposite charge is induced on the paper.

The opposite charges attract, so the paper is attracted to the comb and is lifted upwards, overcoming the gravitational force acting on it.

Electrostatics questions often require friction, electrons, insulators, induction and attraction/repulsion to be mentioned.

This only happens with small pieces of paper where the force of electrostatic attraction is stronger than their weight.

Now try this

1. Describe how a comb can be statically charged if it is plastic but not if it is metal. **(2 marks)**

2. Describe how you can get an electric shock if you touch a door handle. **(5 marks)**

3. Lightning strikes can occur between clouds. Explain how this happens. **(4 marks)**

Electrostatics uses and dangers

Static electricity can be very useful but also very dangerous.

Uses of electrostatics

Static electricity is useful in **paint spraying** and **insecticide** sprayers.

Remember that like charges repel so if all droplets have the same charge the spray will spread out as a fine mist.

Insecticide sprayers

| Nozzle of sprayer is connected to electricity supply | → | Droplets all get the **same kind of** static charge | → | Droplets **repel** each other so the spray spreads out evenly |

Paint sprayers

| Nozzle of sprayer is connected to electricity supply | → | Droplets all get the **same kind** of static charge so they spread out evenly | → | The object being painted is given the **opposite** charge to the paint | → | The paint is attracted to the object being painted and less paint is wasted |

Dangers of electrostatics

When tankers, cars or aircraft move, friction occurs between the body of the vehicle and the air. This results in electrons being transferred and the vehicle becoming charged.

Friction between fuel and the pipe it is flowing through can also cause the transfer of electrons so that the fuel and pipe become charged.

Earthing

If the charge is not removed from an aeroplane or tanker, then a spark may occur when the nozzle of the fuel tanker touches the aeroplane. The spark is an uncontrolled discharge of electrons, and it can ignite fuel vapours and cause an explosion.

Earthing is used to ensure safe movement of electrons off the surface to avoid a dangerous build-up of charge.

An earthing or bonding wire is connected between the aeroplane or fuel tanker and ground before refuelling starts.

Worked example

Electrostatics is used in the spray-painting of cars. The car frame is charged. Suggest how the process works. **(5 marks)**

The paint droplets become charged due to friction and will repel as they all have the same type of charge. The droplets spread out and cover all of the car frame, which has been given the opposite charge. This means that there will be an even coating of paint, and less paint will be wasted.

Worked example

Explain how static electricity can be dangerous when refuelling an aeroplane and how the problem is solved. **(4 marks)**

Aeroplanes become charged due to friction when they fly, as electrons are transferred from the air to the outer casing of the plane. When they land, the charge needs to be removed by taking electrons to the ground with an earthing wire. If this is not done, the charge may cause a spark, which can ignite the fuel vapour, resulting in an explosion.

Now try this

1 Describe how insecticide spray droplets spread out when they are charged. **(2 marks)**

2 Explain the main stages in the use of an electrostatic insecticide spray. **(4 marks)**

3 Explain why charge can be dangerous when refuelling a plane. **(3 marks)**

Electric fields

An **electric field** is a region in space where a **charged particle** may experience a **force**.

Electric field from a point charge

The **electric field** from a **positive point charge** acts **radially outwards**.

The **electric field** from a **negative point charge** acts **radially inwards**.

Electric field strength is a **vector** quantity because it has both a **size** and a **direction**. The arrows show the direction that a **positive charge** would move in if it were placed in the field.

A positive charge in the field around a negative charge would move towards the negative charge, since positive and negative charges attract.

An electric field is created in the region around a charged particle. The charged particle will experience a non-contact force. A negatively charged electron placed in the electric field around a positively charged nucleus will experience a non-contact force that attracts it towards the positive charge. This explains why materials can gain electrons when they are rubbed, and explains why we encounter static electricity in nature.

Only electrons are transferred when an insulator becomes charged. If a material gains electrons it becomes negatively charged; if it loses electrons it becomes positively charged.

Showing the strength of the field

The strength of an electric field is shown by the concentration of the field lines. The more concentrated the lines, the stronger the electric field.

weak positive point charge

weak negative point charge

strong negative point charge

The electric field between parallel plates

The electric field lines between oppositely charged parallel plates are parallel lines.

The more concentrated the field lines, the stronger the electric field.

The field lines are curved at the ends of the plates.

Worked example

Explain what will happen to a proton that is placed in the electric field of a point positive charge. **(3 marks)**

A proton is a positively charged particle, so it will be repelled by the positive charge and move outwards. Since the proton will experience a resultant force, it will accelerate.

Worked example

Describe the path taken by an electron that is placed between oppositely charged parallel plates. **(3 marks)**

The electron is negatively charged and will be repelled by the negative plate and attracted by the positive plate. This will cause it to accelerate towards the positive plate.

Now try this

1 Describe how the motion of a charged particle changes in an electric field when:
   (a) its mass changes   **(2 marks)**

   (b) it is given the opposite charge.   **(2 marks)**
2 Explain how electric fields provide an explanation of static electricity.   **(4 marks)**

Extended response – Static electricity

There will be one or more 6-mark questions on your exam paper. For these questions, you will need to think scientifically and structure your answer logically, showing how the points you make are related to each other. You can revise the topics for this question, which is about **static electricity**, on pages 85–88.

Worked example

An electric field is a region in space where an electric charge experiences a force.

There are two common shapes for an electric field: a radial field around a point charge and the uniform parallel field between metal plates, as shown in the diagrams.

Explain the motion of a positively charged proton in each of these fields.

Your answer should refer to the size and direction of the forces acting on the proton in each of the electric fields shown. **(6 marks)**

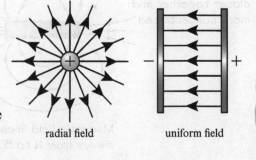

radial field   uniform field

In the case of the radial field, the proton will move away from the positive point charge because like charges repel. Similarly, the proton will move away from the positive plate and towards the negative plate when placed in the region of the uniform field. It will be repelled by the positive plate and attracted by the negative plate.

> In both cases, the direction of the proton's motion is stated, with a simple explanation given based on the nature of repulsion and attraction of charged particles.

The force acting on the proton in the radial field will be radially outwards from the point charge and the size of the force will decrease in magnitude the further the proton moves away from the point charge. This is shown by the fact that the field lines diverge (get further apart) as the distance from the point charge increases. For the uniform field, the force is constant throughout and acts from the positive plate to the negative plate.

> The magnitude of the force on the proton is being related to size of the field as well as the shape and the direction of the field lines.

The acceleration of the proton in the radial field will decrease as it moves further away from the point charge. For the uniform field, the force will be constant throughout as indicated by the parallel lines, so the particle will have a constant acceleration between the plates.

> The relationship between force and acceleration is given by Newton's second law and the equation $F = ma$. If the force acting on the body gets smaller then the acceleration will also get smaller.

You can find out more about the relationship between force and acceleration on page 8.

Now try this

A metal rod, a Perspex rod and a polythene rod can all be rubbed with a cloth.

Explain why certain materials, when rubbed, will attract pieces of tissue paper whereas others will not.

Your answer should refer to the nature of insulators and conductors and the movement of particles when materials become statically charged. **(6 marks)**

Magnets and magnetic fields

Certain materials can be magnetised to become **permanent** or **temporary magnets**.

Magnets and magnetic fields

Like magnetic poles **repel**. Unlike magnetic poles **attract**.

The magnetic field is strongest at the poles. The field lines are shown to be closer together and more concentrated.

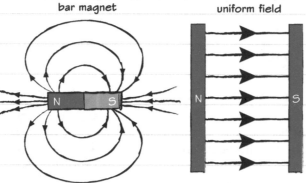

bar magnet   uniform field

Magnetic field lines are always from N to S.

The field is constant. This is shown by parallel, equally spaced field lines.

Permanent and induced magnets

Magnetic materials include **cobalt, steel, iron, nickel** and **magnadur**.

A **permanent magnet** has poles which are N and S all of the time. They are made from steel or magnadur.

A **temporary magnet** can be magnetised by bringing a permanent magnet near to it. When the permanent magnet is removed, the temporary magnet loses its magnetism.

Uses of magnets

Permanent	Temporary
fridge magnets	electromagnets
compasses	circuit breakers
motors and generators	electric bells
loudspeakers	magnetic relays
door closers on fridges	

Plotting compasses

A plotting compass is used to plot the shape and direction of magnetic lines of force. You can do this by laying a bar magnet on a piece of paper. Put the plotting compass by one pole of the magnet. Draw a dot by the needle away from the magnet. Move the plotting compass so that the other point is by the dot you have just drawn. Continue doing this until you have mapped all the way around the magnet.

The Earth's magnetic field has the same pattern as that of a bar magnet and can be plotted using a plotting compass. The behaviour of compasses is evidence that the Earth has a magnetic field.

Worked example

What will the plotting compass needle look like when it is placed at point 1?   **(1 mark)**

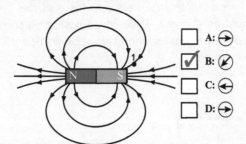

☐ A: ⊕→
✓ B: ⊕↘
☐ C: ←⊕
☐ D: ⊕→

Explain how you can tell if a magnetic material is a permanent or a temporary magnet.   **(2 marks)**

A temporary magnetic material will always be attracted by a magnet, but a permanent magnet can be both attracted and repelled.

A magnadur magnet can be used to do this. Magnadur magnets are ceramic and have their poles on the larger flat faces.

Now try this

1 Draw the field lines for
   (a) a weak bar magnet   **(2 marks)**
   (b) a strong uniform field.   **(2 marks)**

2 Explain why unmagnetised iron is always attracted by a permanent magnet.   **(3 marks)**
3 Describe how a permanent and a temporary magnet are different from each other.   **(3 marks)**

Current and magnetism

An **electric current** will create a **magnetic field**. The **shape, direction** and **strength** of the field depend on a number of factors.

The magnetic field around a long straight conductor

The shape of the magnetic field around a long straight conductor can be thought of as a series of concentric circles.

Be careful! Do not confuse the direction of the current with electron flow. You need to use the direction of conventional current which is taken to be from + to –.

If you point the thumb of your right hand in the direction of the flow of conventional current, the direction that your fingers curl will be the direction of the magnetic field.

The strength of the magnetic field depends on:
- the size of the current in the wire: it is directly proportional to the current.
- the distance from the wire: it is inversely proportional to the distance from the wire.

The direction of the magnetic field depends on the direction of the electric current in the conductor.

You can use plotting compasses or iron filings to show the circular shape of the magnetic field around a current-carrying wire.

The solenoid

The magnetic field lines of the individual coils in a solenoid add up to give a very strong, uniform field along the centre of the solenoid. However, the field lines cancel to give a weaker field outside the solenoid.

Worked example

Explain how the strength of a magnetic field due to a current in a long straight wire changes when:
(a) the current increases   **(1 mark)**

It will increase.

(b) the distance increases.   **(1 mark)**

It will decrease.

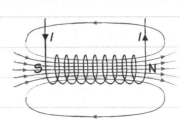

Maths skills **Directly proportional** means that as **one variable increases** the other **variable increases** at **the same rate.** If the current doubles, the magnetic field strength will also double.

Maths skills **Inversely proportional** means that as **one variable increases** the other **decreases.** If the distance doubles, the field strength halves.

Now try this

1. Draw the magnetic field around a wire when the current is flowing downwards.   **(2 marks)**
2. The current flowing in a long straight wire and the distance from the wire are both doubled. Explain what effect this will have on the magnetic field strength.   **(3 marks)**
3. Suggest how the magnetic field strength inside a solenoid could be increased.   **(3 marks)**

Extended response – Magnetism and the motor effect

There will be one or more 6-mark questions on your exam paper. For these questions, you will need to think scientifically and structure your answer logically, showing how the points you make are related to each other. You can revise the topics for this question, which is about **magnetism** and the **motor effect**, on pages 90 and 91.

Worked example

A wire is arranged vertically as shown, with plotting compasses placed around it.

$I = 0$

Explain what happens once a current starts to flow in the wire.

Your answer should refer to what happens when the current, and the distance of the plotting compasses from the wire, are changed, and how the size of the magnetic field would change if measured with a meter. **(6 marks)**

At first, there is no current flowing in the wire, and the plotting compass needles all point in the same direction because they are aligned with the Earth's magnetic field.

When a current flows in a long straight wire, a circular magnetic field is produced around the wire and the compass needles will re-align to point in a circular direction. This will be clockwise if the current is in one direction and will be anticlockwise if the direction of the current is reversed.

The magnetic field will be stronger if the current is increased, and it will be stronger closer to the wire, and get smaller the further away from the wire you go.

Command word: Explain

When you are asked to **explain** something, it is not enough to just state or describe something. Your answer **must** contain some reasoning or justification of the points you make based on the appropriate physics. This needs to be communicated clearly using good spelling, punctuation and grammar.

The answer starts by stating how the compass needles are behaving before any current flows in the wire.

The answer then mentions that a magnetic effect is caused by the current, leading to a circular magnetic field around the wire.

The answer then mentions how changing the current and the distance affects the strength of the magnetic field.

Now try this

Magnetism can be used to attract a variety of materials of different masses. Explain how the strength of the magnetic field can be changed to make this possible. Your answer should refer to how the size of the magnetic field strength can be changed **with** and **without** the use of an **electric current**. **(6 marks)**

Transformers

Transformers can be used to **change the size** of an **alternating voltage** or **current**. Electricity is transmitted across the UK by the National Grid.

Transformers

A transformer can be used to change the potential difference of an alternating electricity supply.

A transformer is made of two coils of insulated wire which are wound onto an iron core. There is no electrical connection between the two coils of wire.

Remember that the **primary coil** is the one connected to the electricity supply.

5 coils   10 coils   secondary coil

10 V ~   INPUT   OUTPUT   Ⓥ 20 V

The National Grid

① **Fossil fuels** or **nuclear fuel** are used to generate electrical energy.

② A **step-up transformer** increases the voltage. For a fixed amount of electrical energy or power output, increasing the voltage means there will be a decrease in current. Electrical energy is transmitted at a high voltage and low current to reduce energy losses as heat in the wires. It also means thinner wires can be used, which reduces costs.

③ **Step-down transformers** decrease the voltages from the National Grid for safer use in our homes and industry. Reducing the voltage means there will be an increase in current.

National Grid system

step-up transformers ②

132 kV or higher

step-down transformers ③

power station

light industry   homes

① 11 kV   230 V

Transformer efficiency

It is assumed that transformers are 100% efficient. They are connected by the equation:

$V_p \times I_p = V_s \times I_s$

| potential difference across primary coil (V) | × | current in primary coil (A) | = | potential difference across secondary coil (V) | × | current in secondary coil (A) |

Worked example

A transformer has a potential difference of 12 V a.c. across its primary coil and a current of 18 A flowing in the primary coil. The potential difference across the secondary coil is 144 V. Calculate the current flowing in the secondary coil. **(4 marks)**

$V_p \times I_p = V_s \times I_s$

$12V \times 18A = 144V \times I_s$

$I_s = 12V \times 18A \div 144V$

$= 1.5A$

Now try this

1 Explain why electrical energy is transmitted at a high voltage and a low current on the National Grid.   **(3 marks)**

2 A transformer has a potential difference of 24 V across the primary coil. The potential difference across the secondary coil is 120 V and the current through it is 0.5 A. Calculate the current in the primary coil.   **(3 marks)**

Extended response – Electromagnetic induction

There will be one or more 6-mark questions on your exam paper. For these questions, you will need to think scientifically and structure your answer logically, showing how the points you make are related to each other. You can revise the topics for this question, which is about **electromagnetic induction**, on page 93.

Worked example

Electrical energy is transferred to consumers by the National Grid. Explain how electrical energy is transferred so that the process is as efficient as possible.

Your answer should refer to any changes in current or potential difference during the transmission of electricity across the UK in the National Grid.

High voltage transmission lines

Consumers, for example homes, factories and shops

Power station   Step-up transformer   Step-down transformer

This electrical power needs to be transmitted to consumers as efficiently as possible, which means that as little power as possible is wasted to the surroundings as thermal energy. Since the equation for electrical power is given by power = current × potential difference, the energy can be transmitted at a high current or at a high potential difference.

The potential difference is increased at the power station by step-up transformers. This means that the potential difference is increased and the current in the transmission lines is decreased so that energy lost by heating is minimised. The greater the current, the more energy is dissipated as thermal energy, so the current is kept low and the potential difference high.

Transformers are designed to be almost 100% efficient since they waste very little energy to the surroundings in the form of thermal energy. Step down transformers are then used to decrease the potential difference to safe, manageable levels in homes. The current increases according to the power equation.

Command word: Explain

When you are asked to explain something, it is not enough to just state or describe something. Your answer must contain some reasoning or justification of the points you make based on the appropriate physics. This needs to be communicated clearly using good spelling, punctuation and grammar.

The answer starts by explaining the role of the National Grid and a quick explanation of the term efficiency. The equation for power is stated, as well as how electrical energy can be transmitted across the UK.

The role of a step-up transformer is explained, as is the principle of conservation of energy or power – there is a fixed amount of power to be transmitted, so if the potential difference increases, the current must decrease so that the amount of power remains constant throughout.

In addition to having an efficient process by having a low current, a mention is made that transformers are designed to be efficient as they waste very little energy when stepping up or stepping down potential differences.

Now try this

Transformers are used to step up and step down potential difference in the transmission of electricity across the UK. Explain how transformers work and why electricity is transmitted at a large voltage and a small current in the transmission lines of pylons.

Your answer should refer to an equation that relates power loss to electric current.

(6 marks)

Changes of state

Substances can change from one state of matter to another. The **change of state** depends on whether **energy is gained** or **lost** by the substance.

The three states of matter

solid

In a solid the particles vibrate but they cannot move freely.

liquid

In a liquid the particles can move past each other and move around randomly.

gas

In a gas the particles move around very fast and they move all the time. This is because they have a lot of **kinetic energy**.

Changing state

Changes of state are **physical** changes rather than chemical changes and they can be reversed.

The mass before the change is equal to the mass after the change. For example, when 500 kg of a solid melts it becomes 500 kg of a liquid.

When a body is heated or cooled, its temperature will change if its state of matter does not change. For example, if 750 ml of a liquid is heated, then the temperature will increase until it reaches its boiling point.

When a material changes state, it does so at a **constant** temperature. For example, when water boils, 1 kg of water at 100°C will turn to 1 kg of steam at 100°C. For more about this, see page 98.

Thermal energy is transferred to the system.

Thermal energy is transferred from the system to the surroundings.

evaporation gas condensation

sublimation liquid desublimation

melting liquid freezing

solid

Worked example

Describe what happens when 2.0 kg of steam is allowed to cool against a glass plate, collected and then placed in a freezer. **(4 marks)**

2.0 kg of water will be produced when the steam turns to water at 100°C. It will then cool as a liquid from 100°C to room temperature. When placed in the freezer it will cool down from room temperature and turn to ice at 0°C before continuing to cool to around −18°C.

Now try this

1 Describe what happens when 1.5 kg of ice is left on a kitchen bench. **(3 marks)**

2 What effect does cooling a gas have on its pressure and volume? **(3 marks)**
3 Describe what happens when 200 kg of solid copper is heated to beyond its boiling point. **(5 marks)**

Density

The **density** of a material is a measure of the **amount of matter** that it contains **per unit volume**.

Density, mass and volume

Changing the amount of material will change **both** its mass and its volume. If the volume of a block of a particular material is doubled, its mass will also double.

The density of a material does not vary greatly for a given state of matter and relates to how closely packed the atoms or molecules are within the volume that it occupies.

The density of a material in the different states of matter varies greatly because of the arrangement of the particles in the state.

solid   liquid   gas

In a **solid**, the particles are closely packed together. The number of particles in a given volume is high.

In a **liquid**, the particles are usually less densely packed than in a solid. The number of particles in a given volume is less than for a solid. Solids are high density.

In a **gas**, the particles are spread out. The number of particles in a given volume is low. Gases are low density.

Calculating density

You can calculate density using the equation:

$$\text{density (kg/m}^3) = \frac{\text{mass (kg)}}{\text{volume (m}^3)}$$

$$\rho = \frac{m}{v}$$

LEARN IT!
IT'S NOT ON THE EQUATIONS LIST

Changing the volume of a substance will change its mass, but its density will be constant.

Other units for density can also be used, such as g/cm^3. The density of copper is $8.96\,g/cm^3$. This means that every $1\,cm^3$ of copper metal has a mass of $8.96\,g$.

Worked example

(a) A body has a mass of $34\,000\,kg$ and a volume of $18\,m^3$. Calculate its density. **(4 marks)**

density = mass ÷ volume
= $34\,000\,kg \div 18\,m^3$
= $1900\,kg/m^3$

(b) Calculate the mass of $0.2\,m^3$ of this material. **(4 marks)**

mass = density × volume
= $1900\,kg/m^3 \times 0.2\,m^3 = 380\,kg$

Maths skills — Using correct units

When performing calculations involving density, mass and volume check that:

☑ you are using the correct equation to find density, mass or volume

☑ the units are consistent.

When the mass is in kg and the volume is in m^3 then the density will be in kg/m^3. Sometimes you may be dealing with g and cm^3, so check the units.

Worked example

A solid has a density of $3.6\,g/cm^3$ and a mass of $320\,g$. Calculate its volume. **(4 marks)**

volume = mass ÷ density
= $320\,g \div 3.6\,g/cm^3 = 88.9\,cm^3$

Maths skills — Checking units

Since volume = mass ÷ density then the units here will be $g \div g/cm^3$. This is the same as $g \times cm^3/g$, which means the grams cancel and we are left with cm^3 – a unit of volume.

Now try this

1 Calculate the density of a material that has a mass of $862\,g$ and a volume of $765\,cm^3$.
(3 marks)

2 The density of aluminium is $2700\,kg/m^3$. Calculate the mass of a block of aluminium with a volume of $50\,000\,cm^3$. **(4 marks)**

Investigating density

Practical skills You can measure the volume and mass of solids and liquids to determine their densities.

Core practical

There is more information about the relationship between mass, volume and density on page 96.

Aim

To determine the density of solids and liquids.

Apparatus

measuring cylinder, displacement can, electronic balance, ruler, various solids and liquids

Be careful to use solids and liquids that are safe to use in this investigation. Mercury (a liquid metal) was used in these investigations until it was found to be carcinogenic.

Method 1 (for a solid)

1 Measure the mass of the solid using an electronic balance and record its mass in your results table.

2 Determine the volume of the solid. This can be done by measuring its dimensions and using a formula, or by using a displacement can to see how much liquid it displaces. Record this value in your results table.

When taking volume readings, make sure that you read the scales with your eye at the same level as the meniscus. Otherwise a parallax error will arise and your values will be incorrect.

Method 2 (for a liquid)

1 Find the mass of the liquid by placing the measuring cylinder on the scales, and then zeroing the scales with no liquid present in the measuring cylinder. Add the liquid to the desired level.

2 Record the mass of the liquid in g from the balance and its volume in cm³ from the measuring cylinder.

Be careful to read the volume value correctly – at the bottom of the meniscus.

Results

Your results can be recorded in a table.

Material	Mass (g)	Volume (cm³)	Density (g/cm³)

3 Find the density of the solid by using the equation density = mass ÷ volume.

Conclusion

The density of a solid and a liquid can be determined by finding their respective masses and volumes. Dividing the mass by the volume gives you the density of the solid or liquid.

Maths skills **Converting between units**

Density can be given in g/cm³ or kg/m³.

Since 1 kg = 1000 g and 1 m³ = 1 000 000 cm³:
- to convert from g/cm³ to kg/m³ multiply by 1000
- to convert from kg/m³ to g/cm³ divide by 1000.

For example, water has a density of 1 g/cm³ or 1000 kg/m³.

Now try this

1 A measuring cylinder is placed on an electronic balance and its display is set to zero. The measuring cylinder is then filled with a liquid up to a volume of 256 cm³. The mass shown is 454 g. Calculate the density of the liquid.
(3 marks)

2 Explain how misreading the mass and volume values may occur and how this can lead to a higher than normal density value. **(4 marks)**

Energy and changes of state

You can calculate how much energy you need to **change the temperature** and **state** of a substance.

Specific heat capacity

Specific heat capacity is the **thermal energy** that must be **transferred** to change the **temperature** of **1 kg** of a material **by 1 °C**. Different materials have different specific heat capacities. Water has a value of 4200 J/kg°C, which means that 1 kg of water needs 4200 J of thermal energy to be transferred to raise its temperature by 1 °C.

You can calculate the thermal energy required using the equation: $\Delta Q = m \times c \times \Delta\theta$

$$\underset{\text{(J)}}{\text{change in thermal energy}} = \underset{\text{(kg)}}{\text{mass}} \times \underset{\text{(J/kg°C)}}{\text{specific heat capacity}} \times \underset{\text{(°C)}}{\text{change in temperature}}$$

Specific latent heat

Specific latent heat is the **energy** that must be transferred to change **1 kg** of a material from one **state of matter to another**. There are usually two values for specific latent heat:

1 the **specific latent heat of fusion** when the change of state is between a solid and a liquid – during **melting** or **freezing**

2 the **specific latent heat of vaporisation** when the change of state is between a liquid and a gas – during **boiling** or **condensation**.

You can calculate the thermal energy required using the equation:

thermal energy for a change of state (J) = mass (kg) × specific latent heat (J/kg)

$$Q = m \times L$$

Specific latent heat should **not** be confused with specific heat capacity. Calculations involving **specific latent heat** involve changes of state and **never involve a change in temperature**, since **changes of state always occur** at a **constant temperature**.

Worked example

(a) A mass of 800 g has a specific heat capacity of 900 J/kg°C and is heated from 20 °C to 80 °C. Calculate how much thermal energy was supplied. **(3 marks)**

$\Delta Q = m \times c \times \Delta\theta$

$0.8 \times 900 \times (80 - 20) = 43\,200\,J$

(b) Calculate the energy required to convert 40 kg of ice at 0 °C to liquid water at 0 °C. The specific latent heat of fusion of water is 334 000 J/kg. **(3 marks)**

$Q = m \times L$

$Q = 40 \times 334\,000 = 13\,360\,000\,J$

Worked example

Ice at –40 °C is heated until it becomes steam at 110 °C. Sketch a graph to show the changes that take place during this process.

Now try this

1 Calculate the energy required to raise the temperature of 15 kg of water from 18 °C to 74 °C. **(3 marks)**

2 Calculate the amount of energy that needs to be supplied to convert 25 kg of ice at 0°C into 25 kg of water at 0°C. **(3 marks)**

Thermal properties of water

 Practical skills You can determine the specific heat capacity of water using an electric heater. You can also observe how water behaves when a sample of ice is melted.

Core practical

> There is more information about specific heat capacity on page 98, and more information about the energy transferred by a known current and potential difference on page 81.

Aim

To determine the specific heat capacity of water and to describe the behaviour of ice when melting.

Apparatus

water, ice, thermometers, electric heater, power supply, insulation, beakers, electronic balance

> Having insulation around the beaker will transfer less energy to the surroundings and give a more accurate value for the specific heat capacity of the water.

Method

1 Set the apparatus up as shown in the diagram.

2 Measure the mass (m) of the water using an electronic balance.

3 Record the potential difference (V) of the power supply and the current (I) through the heater.

4 Take temperature readings every 30 seconds for a time (t) until the water reaches the desired temperature. Record the initial and final temperatures of the water and find the change in temperature (ΔT).

> When recording the temperature readings, avoid parallax errors by reading the thermometer scale at eye level. Record the temperature values regularly, at equal intervals and ensure that the thermometer is in the middle of the liquid.

thermometer

to power supply

electric heater

Results

Plot a graph of temperature against time. Calculate the specific heat capacity. The value c is found by substituting the results into the equation $c = (V \times I \times t) / (m \times \Delta T)$.

> A graph of temperature against time for ice melting to water is shown here.

Conclusion

The specific heat capacity of water is the energy required to change 1 kg of water by a temperature of 1 °C. Its value is about 4200 J/kg °C. Water melts when it changes from ice to liquid water. There is no change in temperature and 1 kg of ice requires 334 000 J to melt.

> The word 'specific' here in this context is for 1 kg of mass. In other words, the values for specific heat capacity and latent heat are for when 1 kg either changes temperature by 1 °C or when it changes state.

Now try this

1 Explain why insulating the beaker leads to a more accurate value for the specific heat capacity of water. **(3 marks)**

2 Describe when
  (a) heating water leads to a change in temperature **(2 marks)**
  (b) heating water does not lead to a change in temperature. **(2 marks)**

3 Draw the apparatus that would allow you to obtain the temperature–time graph of melting ice. **(3 marks)**

Pressure and temperature

The **pressure** of a **gas** can be explained in terms of the motion of its particles.

The pressure of a gas

Gas pressure depends on the motion of the particles in the gas. Gas particles strike the walls of a container at many different angles. So the pressure of a gas produces a net force at right angles to the wall.

Pressure can be increased by:
* **increasing** the **temperature** of the gas
* **increasing** the **mass** of the gas
* **decreasing** the **volume** of the gas.

Pressure and temperature

The **pressure** of a **fixed mass** of **gas** at a **constant volume** depends on the **temperature** of the gas. When the temperature increases:

1. The gas molecules have a greater average kinetic energy.
2. The gas molecules move faster.
3. There are more collisions between the molecules and the walls of the container each second.
4. More force is exerted on the same area each second.
5. The pressure of the gas increases.

Absolute zero

As a gas is cooled the average speed of its particles falls and its volume gets smaller. At −273°C the gas volume shrinks to zero. This temperature is called **absolute zero**. This is the zero temperature on the Kelvin scale. 0 K is equivalent to −273°C.

The temperature of a gas is directly proportional to the average kinetic energy of the gas molecules.

Volume is directly proportional to temperature in Kelvin

To convert between the Kelvin and Celsius scales use the appropriate formula:
* Celsius → Kelvin **add** 273 to the Celsius temperature.
* Kelvin → Celsius **subtract** 273 from the Kelvin temperature.

Worked example

Explain gas pressure using kinetic theory.   **(3 marks)**

The particles (atoms or molecules) in a gas are continuously moving in a random way and colliding with the container walls. The force from these collisions produces pressure on the walls. On average the number and force of collisions is the same in all directions, so pressure is the same on all the walls of the container.

Worked example

Convert
(a) 150°C to Kelvin   **(1 mark)**
150 + 273 = 423K
(b) 150 K to degrees Celsius.   **(1 mark)**
150 − 273 = −123°C

Now try this

1 (a) Convert 20°C to a temperature on the Kelvin scale.   **(1 mark)**
  (b) Convert 300 K to its equivalent temperature on the Celsius scale.   **(1 mark)**
2 The temperature of a gas is doubled from 300 K to 600 K. Explain what happens to the average kinetic energy of the molecules in the gas when this happens.   **(3 marks)**
3 (a) State what happens to the average speed of gas particles as a gas is cooled.   **(1 mark)**
  (b) Explain the effect this has on the pressure of the gas in a rigid sealed container.   **(2 marks)**

Volume and pressure

The **change in the volume** of a gas is **inversely proportional** to the change in pressure when the mass and temperature are constant.

Changing the volume of a gas at constant temperature

Pressure and **volume** are **inversely proportional** to one another.

You can make a gas contract (decrease its volume) by increasing the pressure being exerted.

The product of pressure and volume, P × V, will always have the same value.

10 m³ × 100 kPa = 1 000 000 Pa

5 m³ × 200 kPa = 1 000 000 Pa

Decreasing the volume of a gas at a constant temperature means that the moving gas particles will collide more frequently with the walls of the container they are in. The pressure of the gas will increase.

As the pressure increases then the volume of the gas must decrease if the temperature of the gas is kept constant.

Gas equation

You can use this equation to calculate the pressure or volume of gases for a fixed mass of gas at a constant temperature:

$P_1 \times V_1 = P_2 \times V_2$

The SI units for P are pascals (Pa) and for V are m³.

   $1 \text{ kPa} = 1000 \text{ Pa}$

The units for pressure and volume do not have to be in SI units as long as the same units are used throughout.

See page 106 for more on pressure in a fluid.

Worked example

At atmospheric pressure, 100 kPa, the volume of the column of trapped gas in the apparatus shown is 40 cm³. The pump is used to increase the pressure on the trapped gas to 250 kPa. Calculate the new volume of the trapped air.   **(4 marks)**

$P_1 \times V_1 = P_2 \times V_2$

$100\,000 \text{ Pa} \times 40 \text{ cm}^3 = 250\,000 \text{ Pa} \times V_2)$

so $V_2 = 100\,000 \text{ Pa} \times 40 \text{ cm}^3 \div 250\,000 \text{ Pa}$

$= 16 \text{ cm}^3$

Worked example

A gas at an initial pressure of 102 kPa occupies a volume of 24 m³. The gas is then compressed, at constant temperature, to a new volume of 4.8 m³. Calculate the new pressure of the gas.   **(4 marks)**

$P_1 \times V_1 = P_2 \times V_2$

$102\,000 \text{ Pa} \times 24 \text{ m}^3 = P_2 \times 4.8 \text{ m}^3$

so $P_2 = 102\,000 \text{ Pa} \times 24 \text{ m}^3 \div 4.8 \text{ m}^3$

So $P_2 = 510\,000 \text{ Pa}$ or 510 kPa

Now try this

1 Describe what happens to the molecules in a gas when the pressure on it is increased at constant temperature.   **(3 marks)**

2 If $P_1 = 200 \text{ kPa}$ and $V_1 = 28 \text{ cm}^3$, calculate the new pressure P_2 when the volume is increased to 44.8 cm³.   **(3 marks)**

3 Explain how it is possible for a gas to be
   (a) compressed at a constant temperature
   (b) compressed so that its temperature increases.   **(4 marks)**

Extended response – Density

There will be one or more 6-mark questions on your exam paper. For these questions, you will need to think scientifically and structure your answer logically, showing how the points you make are related to each other. You can revise the topics for this question, which is about the **particle model**, on pages 95–101.

Worked example

A team of investigators has been asked to determine whether rings being sold in a jeweller's shop are made from pure gold or whether they are fake.

Explain how the investigators could determine whether the rings were made from pure gold, which has a density of $19.3\,g/cm^3$.

Your answer should refer to a suitable experimental method that will allow you to determine the density of the material and any equations you would need before use. **(6 marks)**

Density = mass ÷ volume; it is the mass per unit volume of a material. It is fixed for a substance in a given phase of matter.

> The answer starts with a brief explanation of what density is, as well as stating the equation.

To find the mass of a ring, we would put it on the electronic balance and get its mass in grams. To find the volume of the ring, we would lower it into a measuring cylinder of water and find the difference in the volume readings on the measuring cylinder scale. We do this by subtracting the volume reading before the ring has been submerged in the water from the volume reading after the ring has been submerged. This difference in volume is equal to the volume of the ring in cm^3. Dividing the value for the mass of the ring in g by the volume of the ring in cm^3 will get the value for the density of the ring in g/cm^3.

> The method addresses how the mass and volume can be calculated. You could also refer to the use of a displacement can to determine the ring's volume.

If the value obtained for the density is very close to $19.3\,g/cm^3$ then the ring *might be* made from gold. If the density is very different from the value of $19.3\,g/cm^3$ then it is not pure gold.

> The final part of the answer explains how the density value obtained tells you whether the material is gold or not – notice how the answer states that the ring *might be* gold, since you cannot say for definite as other materials may have this density.

When you structure your answer, make sure that you address the question in an order that allows you to deal with each of the points being asked for. Do not just list equations and facts. Communicate to the examiner that you understand how to find the density of the rings and how it will allow you to determine if the rings are real or fake based on the known value for the density of gold.

Now try this

A gas contains many particles moving with random motion in a container of a fixed volume.

Explain how the pressure of a gas can be increased by changing its volume or temperature.

Your answer should refer to energy, forces and the motion of the particles in the gas. **(6 marks)**

Elastic and inelastic distortion

The distortion of a material may be described as being **elastic** or **inelastic** and **requires more than one force.**

Bending, stretching and compressing

compression

Bending requires two forces, one acting clockwise and one acting anticlockwise.

Stretching requires two forces of tension, acting away from each other.

Compression involves two equal forces acting towards one another.

Elastic distortion

Elastic distortion means that a material will return to its original shape when the deforming force is removed.

The stretched elastic bands return to their original shape after the distorting force is removed. They have undergone elastic distortion.

Inelastic distortion

Inelastic distortion means that a material will not return to its original shape when the deforming force is removed.

before   after

This spring has not returned to its original shape after being distorted, so it has undergone inelastic distortion.

Worked example

Describe what this graph shows for a spring that has been stretched. **(3 marks)**

Initially, the relationship between force and extension is linear, so the behaviour of the spring is elastic for smaller forces.

Point P is the elastic limit. For forces applied after this, the relationship is no longer linear and the spring will not return to its original shape – it will exhibit inelastic distortion.

Now try this

1 Explain the types of forces that cause
   (a) stretching **(2 marks)**
   (b) compression. **(2 marks)**

2 Give examples of materials that exhibit
   (a) elastic distortion **(2 marks)**
   (b) inelastic distortion. **(2 marks)**
3 Explain how you would know when a spring has been stretched beyond its elastic limit. **(2 marks)**

Springs

Forces can lead to the **distortion** of **elastic** objects, resulting in **energy** being stored.

Elastic distortion

A force applied to a spring can make it undergo linear elastic distortion. The equation that describes this is:

$$\text{force exerted on a spring (N)} = \text{spring constant (N/m)} \times \text{extension (m)}$$

$$F = k \times x$$

LEARN IT! ITS NOT ON THE EQUATIONS LIST

You can calculate the work done in stretching a spring using the equation:

$$\text{energy transferred in stretching (J)} = 0.5 \times \text{spring constant (N/m)} \times \text{extension}^2 \text{ (m}^2\text{)}$$

$$E = \tfrac{1}{2} \times k \times x^2$$

Force and linear extension

For elastic distortion, **extension** is **directly proportional** to the **force** exerted, **up to the elastic limit**.

The extension is the amount the spring stretches.

extension, x

Worked example

(a) Calculate the force needed to extend a spring of spring constant 20 N/m by 0.25 m.

(3 marks)

Force = spring constant × extension

= 20 N/m × 0.25 m = 5 N

(b) Calculate the total energy stored in the spring.

(4 marks)

energy stored = work done

$E = \tfrac{1}{2}k \times x^2$

= $\tfrac{1}{2}$ × 48 N/m × (0.25 m)² = 1.5 J

When calculating the spring constant, work done or energy stored, ensure that force is in N and extension is in m.

Always use the extension. You may need to calculate this:

$$\text{extension} = \frac{\text{total stretched length}}{} - \text{original length}$$

Force–extension graph

The gradient tells you the value of the spring constant, k. This is only true when the spring is showing elastic behaviour, i.e. when the line is straight.

elastic limit

Force (N)

Extension (mm)

The area beneath a force-extension graph tells you the energy stored in the spring.

The area under the graph is the area of a triangle $= \tfrac{1}{2} \times F \times x$

The force is given by the equation $F = k \times x$

Substituting this into the equation gives

$E = \tfrac{1}{2} \times k \times x \times x = \tfrac{1}{2}k \times x^2$

Now try this

1 (a) Calculate the force that is required to extend a spring of spring constant 30 N/m by 0.2 m. **(3 marks)**

(b) Calculate how much work is done on the spring under these conditions. **(3 marks)**

2 Describe how the value of the spring constant tells you how easy or difficult it is to cause a spring to extend. **(3 marks)**

3 Calculate how much elastic potential energy is stored in a spring of spring constant 45 N/m when it has an extension of 10 cm. **(4 marks)**

Forces and springs

Practical skills It is possible to determine the extension of a spring, and the work done, by applying different forces to the spring and then plotting a graph.

Core practical

Aim

To determine the extension and work done when applying forces to a spring.

Apparatus

eye protection, spring, ruler, weights, retort stand, boss, clamp

Method

Arrange the apparatus as shown, with the ruler placed vertically alongside the spring and parallel to it. Add masses or weights and collect enough values to plot a graph of force against extension.

spring · ruler · weights

Results

Taking readings for force and extension allows a force-extension graph to be plotted:

Force (N) against Extension (mm)

Conclusion

The gradient of the linear part of a force-extension graph gives you the value for the spring constant of the spring when it behaves elastically. The area beneath the graph equals the work done or the energy stored in the spring as elastic potential energy.

> Wear eye protection when taking readings. A stretched spring stores a lot of elastic energy and this could damage your eyes if released.

> When taking readings of the extension, read the values on the ruler at eye level to avoid parallax errors.

Weight and mass

Weight is a force, not a mass. A mass of 100 g is equivalent to a weight or force of 1 N.

Extension is equal to

$$\text{new length} - \text{original length}$$
$$(m) \qquad\qquad (m)$$

Work done is equal to the energy stored in the spring.

The gradient of a force–extension graph gives you the spring constant.

The area beneath the line is the work done, or the energy stored as elastic potential energy, by the spring.

Maths skills You will need to convert extension values from mm to m before you can calculate an energy value, and state the result in joules, J. Forces also need to be stated in N, so any mass values recorded need to be converted from g to N.

Now try this

1　Calculate the energy stored by a spring of spring constant 5 N/m when extended by 0.5 m.　**(3 marks)**

2　Explain if and how the spring constant and the amount of energy stored can be calculated for springs that are being *compressed*.　**(3 marks)**

Pressure

Pressure is **force** acting per unit **area**. **Fluids** (liquids and gases) exert pressure, which depends on the **depth** and **density** of the fluid.

Pressure

Pressure is the force acting per unit area, measured at right angles to the area. Pressure is measured in pascals (Pa):

$1\,Pa = 1\,N/m^2$.

You can use this equation to calculate pressure:

$$\text{pressure (Pa)} = \frac{\text{force normal to surface (N)}}{\text{area of surface } (m^2)}$$

$P = \dfrac{F}{A}$ **LEARN IT!** ITS NOT ON THE EQUATIONS LIST

(a) A force of 100 N acts normal to a block of wood of area $0.1\,m^2$ in contact with the floor. Calculate the pressure exerted. **(3 marks)**

$P = F \div A$
$\quad = 100\,N \div 0.1\,m^2 = 1000\,Pa$

(b) The wooden block is turned on its end. The area in contact with the floor is now $0.01\,m^2$. Calculate the pressure exerted now. **(3 marks)**

$P = F \div A$
$\quad = 100\,N \div 0.01\,m^2 = 10000\,Pa$

(c) Explain why the pressure has increased. **(3 marks)**

Same force, smaller area, so pressure is greater.

Pressure and depth

The pressure exerted in a liquid will increase with depth. This is because the further down you go in the liquid, the greater the weight of liquid there will be above.

The pressure in a fluid causes a force that is normal to any surface. This means that the force is at right angles or perpendicular to the surface on which it acts.

Pressure and density

The pressure exerted at a given depth in a liquid depends on the density of the liquid. A greater density means more weight will be acting downwards from above that depth.

The pressure exerted by the water is greater than the pressure exerted by the cooking oil from the same height, h, because the water has a higher density.

Atmospheric pressure

The atmosphere can be thought of as a very high column of air above our bodies. It exerts a pressure due to its weight, which acts normal to an area, A.

The further up you go in the Earth's atmosphere,

the less air there will be above you in the column of air – so there is less weight of air above you, hence less pressure, the higher up you go.

The pressure acting on a diver who is 18 m below the surface is 180 kPa due the water above him and 100 kPa due to atmospheric pressure. Calculate the total pressure acting on the diver.

Total pressure = pressure due to the water + pressure due to atmospheric pressure

Total pressure = 180 kPa + 100 kPa
$\qquad\qquad\quad = 280\,kPa$

106

1 Calculate the pressure when a force of 600 N acts over an area of $2.5\,m^2$. **(3 marks)**
2 Explain what affects the total pressure acting on a body that is placed in a fluid. **(3 marks)**

Extended response –
Forces and matter

There will be one or more 6-mark questions on your exam paper. For these questions, you will need to think scientifically and structure your answer logically, showing how the points you make are related to each other. You can revise the topics for this question, which is about **forces and matter**, on pages 103–106.

Worked example

A student performs an investigation to compare the behaviour of two different springs. The force–extension graph for these springs is shown on the right. Compare the springs by using information from the graph. Your answer should refer to the spring constants of the springs, the energy they store and the elastic or inelastic nature of their behaviour. **(6 marks)**

The force–extension graph shows two springs that have both been extended with a maximum load of 29 N. Spring A produces the greater gradient, so it has a higher spring constant than spring B. This means that spring A requires a greater force to extend it by the same amount. Spring A has a spring constant of 500 N/m whereas spring B has a spring constant of 375 N/m.

Spring A behaves elastically throughout as the gradient is constant throughout the experiment because the extension is directly proportional to the force applied. Spring B behaves elastically up to a load force of about 25 N, at which point it starts to behave inelastically. This is shown by the reduction in gradient as the force leads to a greater and greater extension as the layers of atoms slide further apart. Upon removal of the load, spring A will return to its original shape but spring B will not – it will remain extended.

The energy stored by the springs is calculated by using the equation $E = \frac{1}{2} \times k \times x^2$. For the same extension, x, spring A will store a greater elastic potential energy due to its higher spring constant. For an extension of 4 cm, spring A will store 0.4 J whereas spring B will store only 0.3 J.

The answer starts with a quick explanation of what the graph shows. The gradient tells you the spring constant.
For spring A it is 25 N ÷ 0.05 m = 500 N/m and for spring B it is 22.5 ÷ 0.06 m or 375 N/m. Note that the extension has been converted to metres for the calculation: 5 cm = 0.05 m and 6 cm = 0.06 m.

After discussing the spring constant values, the answer then focuses on the elastic and inelastic nature of the springs, using values from the graph and giving an explanation as to what will happen to the springs.

Finally, the answer addresses the energy stored in each of the springs. Notice how the extension has to be converted into m to do the calculation.
4 cm = 0.04 m, so
for spring A, $E = \frac{1}{2} \times 500 \, N/m \times (0.04 \, m)^2 = 0.4$ J
for spring B, $E = \frac{1}{2} \times 375 \, N/m \times (0.04 \, m)^2 = 0.3$ J

Now try this

Describe the difference between elastic and inelastic distortion and explain how the spring constant of a spring and the elastic potential energy it stores can be determined when it is behaving elastically. Your answer should refer to any graph, or equations, that may be useful. **(6 marks)**

Answers

1. Key concepts

1   (a) 3 **(1)** (b) 4 **(1)** (c) 5 **(1)**
2   (a) $12 \times 60 \times 60$ **(1)** $= 43\,200\,\text{s}$ **(1)**
    (b) $= 17.8\,\text{m/s}$ **(1)**
3   $58.3\,\text{MW} = 58\,300\,000\,\text{W}$ **(1)** $= 5.83 \times 10^7\,\text{W}$ **(1)**
4   1.0 **(1)** $\times 10^{-10}\,\text{m}$ **(1)**

2. Scalars and vectors

1   (a) A quantity that has a size or a magnitude only **(1)**. (b) A quantity that has a size or magnitude and a direction **(1)**.
2   (a) **C** mass **(1)** (b) **D** electric field **(1)**
3   (a) $4\,\text{m/s}$ **(1)** (b) $-4\,\text{m/s}$ **(1)**

3. Speed, distance and time

1   speed $= 120\,\text{m} \div 8\,\text{s}$ **(1)**, speed $= 15$ **(1)** m/s **(1)**
2   Distance $=$ average speed $\times$ time **(1)**, $= 9\,\text{m/s} \times 30\,\text{m} = 270$ **(1)** m **(1)**
3   gradient of zero at origin **(1)**, increasing gradient of graph shown **(1)**, distance and time shown as correct y- and x-axes, respectively **(1)**

4. Equations of motion

1   $a = (8\,\text{m/s} - 2\,\text{m/s}) \div 5\,\text{s}$ **(1)** $= 6\,\text{m/s} \div 5\,\text{s} = 1.2$ **(1)** m/s² **(1)**
2   Acceleration $=$ change in velocity $\div$ time taken **(1)** $= (18\,\text{m/s} - 6\,\text{m/s}) \div 4\,\text{s} = 3$ **(1)** m/s² **(1)**
3   Final velocity² – initial velocity² $= 2 \times$ acceleration $\times$ distance **(1)**
    Final velocity² – $(5\,\text{m/s})^2 = 2 \times 2.0\,\text{m/s}^2 \times 180\,\text{s}$ **(1)**
    Final velocity² $= 720 + 25 = 745$ **(1)**
    Final velocity $= \sqrt{745} = 27.3\,\text{m/s}$ **(1)**

5. Velocity/time graphs

1   (a) Gradient of a velocity/time graph gives acceleration. **(1)**
    (b) Area beneath a velocity/time graph gives distance travelled **(1)**.
2   Distance on y-axis, time on x-axis **(1)**, 200 m shown as covered after 8 s **(1)**, 300 m shown as total distance after 13 s **(1)**, axes units given as m on y-axis and s on x-axis **(1)**.
3   (a) Velocity in m/s plotted on y-axis, time in s plotted on x-axis **(1)**, diagonal line from origin to 10 m/s after 4 s drawn **(1)**, horizontal line at 10 m/s for the next 8 s drawn **(1)**, axes units given as m/s on y-axis and s on x-axis **(1)**.
    (b) Distance is area beneath the graph. Area for first 10 s $= \frac{1}{2} \times 10 \times 4 = 20\,\text{m}$ **(1)**, area for the next 8 s is $10\,\text{m/s} \times 8\,\text{s} = 80\,\text{m}$ **(1)**, total distance run $= 80\,\text{m} + 20\,\text{m} = 100\,\text{m}$ **(1)**.

6. Determining speed

1   time taken **(1)** for the object to travel over a known distance **(1)**
2   Light gates do not introduce a human reaction time or human error **(1)** which would increase the actual time value and they can measure to a higher degree of accuracy and to a smaller fraction of a second **(1)**.
3   The trolley will accelerate **(1)** due to the component of its weight acting down the slope **(1)** and this means that the speed increases with time/distance travelled **(1)**.

7. Newton's first law

1   balanced or equal and opposite **(1)** OR no forces acting **(1)**
2   The forces acting on the moving body are in different/opposite directions **(1)** of different sizes **(1)**, or a diagram drawn to show this. These forces could be antiparallel or even at an angle, such as at 90° to the initial movement. A change in direction will occur if the forces oppose the original motion or act in a way to change the direction.
3   diagrams showing: (a) equal forces of 100 N **(1)** and opposite **(1)** or no forces shown; (b) equal forces of 100 N **(1)** and opposite forces **(1)** shown; (c) two forces of 100 N **(1)** both acting to the left **(1)**

8. Newton's second law

1   $F = 1.2\,\text{kg} \times 8\,\text{m/s}^2$ **(1)** $= 9.6$ **(1)** N **(1)**
2   Force $=$ mass $\times$ acceleration, so mass $=$ force $\div$ acceleration **(1)**, $= 24\,\text{N} \div 2\,\text{m/s}^2$ **(1)** $= 12\,\text{kg}$ **(1)**
3   Force $=$ mass $\times$ acceleration, so acceleration $=$ force $\div$ mass **(1)**, $= 6000\,\text{N} \div 1200\,\text{kg}$ **(1)**, $= 5\,\text{m/s}^2$ **(1)**.

9. Weight and mass

1   (a) weight $= 50\,\text{kg} \times 10\,\text{N/kg}$ **(1)** $= 500\,\text{kg}$ **(1)**
    (b) weight $= 50\,\text{kg} \times 26\,\text{N/kg}$ **(1)** $= 1300\,\text{N}$ **(1)**
2   Weight $=$ mass $\times$ g, so mass $=$ weight $\div$ g **(1)**, mass $= 480\,\text{N} \div 10\,\text{N/kg}$ **(1)**, $= 48\,\text{kg}$ **(1)**
3   $g = W \div m$ **(1)** $= 54\,\text{N} \div 18\,\text{kg}$ **(1)** $= 3\,\text{N/kg}$ **(1)**

10. Core practical – Force and acceleration

1   More accurate/repeat readings **(1)** can be taken with little or no human error **(1)** and calculations can be performed quickly by the data logger to provide speeds and accelerations, etc. **(1)**.
2   more accurate mass **(1)**, more accurate slope/gradient **(1)**, reduce friction, more readings for mass **(1)**, repeat readings to determine the precision **(1)**
3   constant mass throughout/other variables controlled **(1)**, change slope by 10° at a time **(1)**, same starting point along slope **(1)**, record enough values for change in velocity and change in times between two light gates **(1)**, repeat readings to determine the precision **(1)**

11. Newton's third law

1   The forces pairs acting on a body have the same size **(1)**, act in opposite directions **(1)** and act on different bodies **(1)**.
2   A force from the ball acts on the gloves **(1)**, an equal and opposite force **(1)** acts from the gloves on the ball **(1)**.

12. Human reaction time

1 (a) Human reaction time is the time between a stimulus occurring and a response (1). (b) any three of: tiredness (1), alcohol (1), drugs (1), distractions (1), age (1).

2 Reaction time = $\sqrt{2 \times distance \div g}$ (1) = $\sqrt{2 \times 0.24\,m \div 10\,m/s^2}$ (1), = 0.22 s (1)

13. Stopping distance

1 Thinking distance (1) and braking distance (1)

2 Thinking distance increases by a factor of four (1), braking distance increases by a factor of 16 (1).

14. Extended response – Motion and forces

*Answer could include the following points:

- reaction times and thinking distance. As reaction time increases so does thinking distance. Reaction time is the time between seeing the hazard and applying a force to the brakes.
- speed of car – affecting thinking and braking distance. More speed means a greater distance is covered when thinking and braking compared with a lower speed.
- alcohol, drugs or tiredness affecting reaction times and thinking distance – both will increase if drivers are under the influence of these since they will be less alert.
- condition of tyres – bald tyres means greater braking distance as there will be less grip.
- condition of road (icy or wet) resulting in less grip.
- mass of car/number of passengers increases braking distance at a given speed due to greater inertial mass/constant force needed over a longer time to stop.

15. Energy stores and transfers

1 Energy store diagram should include the chemical energy, kinetic energy and gravitational potential energy stores and the thermal energy store shown as the wasted form. At each part of the journey of the car uphill, the total of these four stores should be constant. The diagram should show

chemical store → (mechanical) → kinetic store
(decreases)   (energy transfer)   (increases)

+ gravitational potential store + thermal store
    (increases)   (increases)

(4)

2 The kinetic energy store of the car increases (1). The force transfers energy to this store (1). Some of the energy is transferred to the environment by friction with the air and tyres with the road (1) and stored as thermal energy (1).

16. Efficient heat transfer

1 efficiency = (14 J ÷ 20 J) × 100% (1) = 0.7 or 70% (1)

2 Increase the thickness of the wall (1) and use a material with a lower thermal conductivity (1).

17. Energy resources

1 (a) Diagram should show gpe → kinetic → electrical → (thermal energy as wasted). (3)

(b) Diagram should show chemical → heat or ... chemical → electrical or ... chemical → kinetic. (3)

2 biofuels advantages: reliable, can be replaced, can be readily grown and converted to fuels for use in cars, can be stored, renewable, cheap (any 1 for 1 mark); biofuels disadvantages: gives off CO_2/greenhouse gases when burned, not renewable if not regrown (any 1 for 1 mark); solar advantages: renewable, almost infinite energy supply, no cost for the solar energy (any 1 for 1 mark); solar disadvantages: solar cells are expensive to make and buy, unreliable (when not sunny or at night), difficult

to store the energy in electrical form, production of cells in manufacturing will pollute (any 1 for 1 mark)

18. Patterns of energy use

1 two of: threats to food supplies for those who need them (1), global warming and floods due to using fossil fuels (1), running out of non-renewable resources (1)

2 Wood has been readily available (1) for thousands of years (1) and has not had to be discovered, mined or have any extra technology developed (e.g. nuclear reactors/power stations) in order for it to be used to produce thermal energy (1).

19. Potential and kinetic energy

1 $\Delta GPE = m \times g \times \Delta h = 5\,kg \times 10\,N/kg \times 18\,m$ (1) = 900 (1) J (1)

2 Kinetic energy = $\frac{1}{2} \times mass \times velocity^2 = \frac{1}{2} \times 60\,kg \times (5\,m/s)^2$ (1) = 750 (1) J (1)

3 30 km/h = 30 000 m ÷ 3600 s = 8.3 m/s (1), KE = $\frac{1}{2} \times 80\,kg \times 8.3\,m/s$ (1) = 2778 (1) J (1)

20. Extended response – Conservation of energy

*Answer could include the following points (for all six marks, two advantages and two disadvantages with good supporting explanation should be supplied):

- advantages of wind – renewable, no fuel needed, no carbon dioxide gas emissions
- disadvantages – unsightly, unreliable
- advantages of coal – efficient, reliable
- disadvantages – non-renewable, carbon dioxide and sulfur dioxide gas emissions

21. Waves

1 (a) amplitude (1)   wavelength (1)   for correct shape (1)

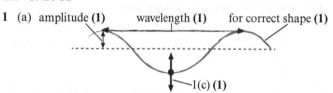

(b) ← or → (1) (c) arrow shown above

2 A particle moves backwards and forwards about a fixed position (1) and parallel to the direction of energy transfer (1).

3 2.2 mm (1) *Any answer between 2.1 and 2.4 is acceptable.*

22. Wave equations

1 (a) Wave speed = frequency × wavelength = 100 Hz × 3.3 m (1) = 330 (1) m/s (1). (b) Wavelength = wave speed ÷ frequency = 330 m/s ÷ 1650 Hz (1) = 0.2 (1) m (1).

2 1 minute = 60 seconds (1); $x = 25\,m/s \times 60\,s$ (1) = 1500 (1) m (1)

23. Measuring wave velocity

1 Wave speed = distance ÷ time = 30 m ÷ 5 s (1) = 6 (1) m/s (1)

2 wave speed = frequency × wavelength = 4 Hz × 0.08 m (1) = 0.32 (1) m/s (1)

3 Make a sound that is a large, known distance away from a wall (1). Find the time between the generation of the sound and the detection of the reflected sound/echo accurately (1). Use the equation total distance travelled ÷ total time (1) to find the speed. Use equipment that has high accuracy for measuring distance and time (1).

24. Waves and boundaries

1 They can be reflected, refracted, transmitted or absorbed **(2 marks for all four, 1 mark for three)**.

2 The sound wave can change its direction **(1)** and its speed **(1)** and it will slow down as sound waves travel faster in warmer air than cooler air **(1)**.

25. Core practical – Waves in fluids

1 Wave speed = distance travelled ÷ time taken **(1)**; wave speed = frequency × wavelength **(1)**

2 As wave speed = frequency × wavelength **(1)**, wavelength increases and frequency stays the same **(1)** so the wave velocity will increase **(1)**.

26. Extended response – Waves

*Answer could include the following points:

- Water wave or sound wave generated.
- Object placed on water wave or in the region of the sound waves.
- Object does not move in direction of wave when wave is generated
- but will move up or down on the water wave,
- backwards and forwards in the sound wave.
- Suitable equipment suggested.

27. Reflection and refraction

1 angle of reflection = angle of incidence = 42° **(1)**

2 greater than 34° **(1)** as it speeds up and bends away from the normal **(1)**

3 Light ray may change direction **(1)** and bend away from normal **(1)** as it moves from glass to air if angle of incidence is not along the normal. There will be no change in direction if the light ray moves into air from glass along the normal **(1)**.

28. Total internal reflection

1 The angle above which light will be reflected back into a material **(1)** when travelling from a more dense to a less dense transparent material (e.g. from water to air or from glass to air) **(1)**.

2 The angle of incidence is greater than the critical angle for the two materials that are in contact **(1)**, so all of the light **(1)** will be totally internally reflected **(1)**.

3 Light needs to travel from a denser material **(1)** to a less dense material **(1)** and angle of incidence needs to be above the critical angle **(1)**.

29. Colour of an object

1 Specular reflection involves the reflection of parallel rays from a smooth surface **(1)** and diffuse reflection is the reflection of rays that will not be parallel, often from a rough surface hence it is diffuse reflection from a gravel path **(1)**.

2 Red light is let through the filter (transmitted) **(1)** and all of the other colours are absorbed **(1)**.

3 White light is composed of wavelengths of different colours **(1)** which will all be absorbed by the blue surface apart from blue light **(1)** which will be reflected **(1)**.

30. Lenses and power

1 The more curved the glass surface is **(1)**, the greater the power of the lens **(1)**.

2 As the power increases, the focal length decreases – or the reverse argument **(1)**.

3 The material/type of glass or plastic/density of glass or plastic that the lens is made from **(1)**.

31. Real and virtual images

1 a real image **(1)**

2 Lens and axis shown with object at 3F **(1)**, construction lines shown **(1)**, virtual image between F and 2F on the other side of the lens from the object **(1)**.

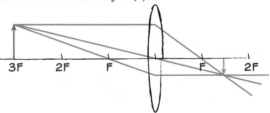

32. Electromagnetic spectrum

1 (a) radio waves **(1)**, (b) gamma-rays **(1)**

2 Wave speed = frequency × wavelength = 3000 m × 100 000 Hz **(1)** = 300 000 000 **(1)** m/s **(1)**

3 Wave speed = frequency × wavelength, so frequency = wave velocity ÷ wavelength **(1)**, = 300 000 000 m/s ÷ 0.05 m **(1)** = 6×10^9 **(1)** Hz **(1)**

33. Core practical – Investigating refraction

1 its speed **(1)**, its direction **(1)**

2 angles of refraction are less than their corresponding angles of incidence **(1)**; angles of refraction are greater than the corresponding angles of refraction for those in the glass block. **(1)**

3 (a) Frequency does not change **(1)** because the frequency is determined by the oscillating source that produces the wave and remains constant regardless of any change in speed or wavelength **(1)**. (b) Wavelength decreases **(1)** because the wave speed decreases and the frequency remains constant **(1)**.

34. EM radiation and temperature

1 The temperature/surface temperature of the body that is emitting the radiation **(1)**.

2 The intensity of the radiation from the pan of water will be greater than the ice **(1)** as it is at a higher temperature **(1)**.

3 Stars are at different temperatures **(1)** and hotter stars emit peak wavelengths that are shorter wavelengths and appear blue **(1)** whereas cooler stars emit peak wavelengths that are longer **(1)** and appear red **(1)**.

35. Core practical – Thermal energy and surfaces

1 Curves will be, in order of steepness, silver **(1)**, white **(1)**, shiny black **(1)**, dull black **(1)**, as shiny is the worst emitter and dull black is the best emitter.

2 The rate **(1)** at which a hot body loses thermal energy **(1)** is directly related to its temperature **(1)**, so a constant, fixed temperature is needed at the start so that a fair test can be established for comparisons **(1)**.

36. Dangers and uses

1 They can cause damage to the skin such as sunburn **(1)**, skin cancer **(1)** as well as damage to the eyes **(1)**.

2 X-rays are useful to doctors as they allow them to detect broken bones **(1)** but can damage cells **(1)**, which could cause them to mutate/lead to cancer **(1)**.

3 Gamma-rays can pass through the body and be detected by, e.g., a gamma camera, allowing a doctor to see if cancer is present **(1)**. Gamma-rays may cause cancer, but this is a risk worth taking if there is a possibility that the patient has a malignant cancer which may lead to death if not detected **(1)**.

37. Changes and radiation

1 Electron energy levels or shells **(1)** and in the nucleus **(1)**.

2 (a) Electrons move to higher energy levels **(1)** with the difference in energy between the levels equal to the energy of the electromagnetic radiation **(1)**. (b) An electron falls down from a higher to a lower energy level **(1)** with a photon emitted having with energy equal to the energy difference between the two levels **(1)**.

38. Extended response – Light and the electromagnetic spectrum

*Answer could include the following points:

- radio waves: including broadcasting, communications and satellite transmissions
- microwaves: including cooking, communications and satellite transmissions
- infrared: including cooking, thermal imaging, short-range communications, optical fibres, television remote controls and security systems
- visible light: including vision, photography and illumination
- ultraviolet: including security marking, fluorescent lamps, detecting forged bank notes and disinfecting water
- X-rays: including observing the internal structure of objects, airport security scanners and medical X-rays
- gamma-rays: including sterilising food and medical equipment, and the detection of cancer and its treatment

39. Structure of the atom

(a) Diameter of atom ÷ diameter of nucleus = $10^{-10} \div 10^{-15}$ **(1)** = 10^5 or 100 000 times **(1)**.

(b) Diameter of molecule/diameter of nucleus = $10^{-9} \div 10^{-15}$ **(1)** = 10^6 or 1 000 000 times **(1)**.

40. Atoms and isotopes

1 Atoms A and B are isotopes **(1)** as they both contain the same number of protons **(1)**.

2 $^{11}_{5}$B **(1)**

41. Atoms, electrons and ions

1 (a) nucleus **(1)** (b) nucleus **(1)** (c) in orbits or shells around the nucleus **(1)**

2 Atoms of an element contain the same number of protons as electrons **(1)** and have a neutral charge overall **(1)**, whereas ions of an element have the same number of protons but can gain electrons so that they have a negative charge (more electrons than protons) **(1)** or lose electrons so that they have a positive charge (more protons than electrons) **(1)**.

3 (a) A charge of +2 **(1)** as two negative electrons of charge –1 each have been lost **(1)**. (b) A charge of –1 **(1)** as it has gained an electron of charge –1 **(1)**.

42. Ionising radiation

1 Alpha particles/radiation **(1)**

2 You cannot predict **(1)** when a nucleus will decay by emitting radiation **(1)**.

43. Background radiation

1 D medical X-rays **(1)**

2 Low level radiation **(1)** that is present all around us **(1)** and comes from natural and man-made sources **(1)**.

3 (a) The sector for radon would be much smaller **(1)**. (b) The sector for radon would be bigger **(1)**.

44. Measuring radioactivity

1 dosimeter/film badge **(1)**, Geiger–Muller tube **(1)**

2 Lead sheet stops alpha and beta radiation but some gamma will penetrate it **(1)**, gamma is dangerous to the body from an external source **(1)** so the worker knows that they have been exposed to it and needs to seek help **(1)**.

45. Models of the atom

1 Plum pudding model with negative plums in a positive 'dough' **(1)**. Rutherford atom model with a small positive nucleus compared to overall atomic diameter **(1)**. Bohr model with electrons orbiting a positive nucleus in definite, discrete energy levels **(1)**.

2 Positive alpha particles were fired at nucleus **(1)**. Most went through undeflected **(1)**, so most of the atom must be empty space **(1)** and there is a small nucleus as only a very few alpha particles bounced back **(1)**.

3 Evidence **(1)** is collected from experiments **(1)** and if this shows that the new model is better than a previous model it will be accepted as a better model by scientists **(1)**.

46. Beta decay

1 (a) A neutron turns into a proton **(1)** and an electron is emitted **(1)**. (b) A proton turns into a neutron **(1)** and a positron is emitted **(1)**.

2 A beta particle is an electron that is emitted from an unstable nucleus **(1)** and an electron in a stable atom is found in shells orbiting the nucleus **(1)**.

3 $^{66}_{28}$Ni **(1)** $\rightarrow$ $^{66}_{29}$Cu **(1)** + $^{0}_{-1}$e **(1)**, beta minus decay **(1)**

47. Radioactive decay

1 (a) $^{10}_{6}$C $\rightarrow$ $^{10}_{5}$B + $^{0}_{1}$e **(1)**, beta plus decay **(1)**

(b) $^{232}_{90}$Th $\rightarrow$ $^{228}_{88}$Ra + $^{4}_{2}$He **(1)**, alpha decay **(1)**

2 (a) Mass number = 92 + 146 = 238 **(1)**, atomic number is the number of protons = 92 **(1)**.

(b) An alpha particle has a mass of 4 and an atomic number of 2 **(1)** so losing two alpha particles means the mass number decreases by 8 and the atomic number by 4 **(1)**, a beta particle being emitted causes the mass number to stay the same and the atomic number to go up by 1 **(1)**, so the final mass number will be 230 and the atomic number will be 89 **(1)**.

48. Half-life

1 (a) it will halve **(1)** to a value of 2000 Bq **(1)**, (b) it will halve from the 2 day rate of 2000 Bq **(1)** to 1000 Bq **(1)**, (c) it will quarter from the 4 day rate of 1000 Bq **(1)** to 250 Bq **(1)**.

2 120 Bq to 30 Bq is one quarter of the activity or two half-lives in 4 hours **(1)**, so one half-life is half of four hours or 2 hours **(1)**.

3 After 15 minutes: $\frac{1}{2}$; after 30 minutes: $\frac{1}{4}$ **(1)**; after 45 minutes: $\frac{1}{8}$ **(1)**; after 60 minutes: $\frac{1}{16}$ **(1)**.

49. Uses of radiation

1 Any three of sterilising surgical equipment, killing cancer cells, preserving fruit, smoke alarms, thickness testing, X-ray photographs, etc. **(1 mark for each)**.

2 Contains alpha particles **(1)**, which have a short range in air **(1)**, cannot reach body **(1)**.

3 Some medical instruments are damaged by heating them **(1)** but they still need to be sterilised to kill microbes/bacteria **(1)**.

50. Dangers of radiation

1 two of: can cause cells to become ionised, which leads to chemical reactions taking place in cells **(1)** causing them to die **(1)** or mutate **(1)**, which can lead to cancer **(1)**

2 Ionising radiation knocks electrons from shells **(1)** making them more reactive and allowing change to DNA to occur **(1)**,

whereas non-ionising radiation cannot do this as there is not enough energy to knock electrons from shells **(1)**.

3 Minimise the time they are exposed to the radiation **(1)**, wear protective clothing (e.g. lead apron) **(1)**, increase the distance from the radioactive source to the person **(1)**.

51. Contamination and irradiation

1 (a) Irradiation is the exposure of the body to ionising radiation **(1)** from a source that is outside the body **(1)**.

(b) Contamination is exposure to ionising radiation from a source that is taken into the body **(1)** by eating, breathing in, drinking, injection or via contact ionising radiation on the surface of the skin **(1)**.

2 Alpha particles are highly ionising due to their charge and mass **(1)** and will cause damage inside the body as they have a short range **(1)** and will come into contact with cells. Outside the body they are unlikely to reach the body as they have a range of only 5 cm in air and so cannot easily reach the body to cause any ionisation in cells **(1)**.

3 Some sources of background radiation do not come into contact with the body such as cosmic rays from the Sun and medical X-rays **(1)**, but other sources such as radon gas and radioisotopes in food are taken into the body **(1)**.

52. Medical uses

1 A radioisotope that is taken into the body (by injection or eating/drinking it) **(1)**. It is used to monitor biological processes in the body **(1)**

2 A single high-energy beam would have a much higher energy **(1)** so that it would destroy all cells it came into contact with when fired at the body **(1)**, whereas many low-energy beams will not have sufficient photon energy by themselves to harm healthy cells **(1)** but when they are focused at a point the energies of the individual beams add up to become a large energy that can kill the cancer tumour **(1)**.

3 Gamma rays can penetrate the body **(1)** and be detected by a detector outside the body **(1)** and are not absorbed by cells (unlike alpha particles) so do not damage cells by ionising atoms **(1)**.

53. Nuclear power

1 Energy is needed to build **(1)** and decommission **(1)** nuclear power stations, so unless all this energy comes from nuclear power stations (or renewable resources) some carbon dioxide will be added to the atmosphere from burning fossil fuels **(1)**.

2 any four from: nuclear radiation in the form of gamma-rays **(1)** can escape from nuclear power stations in small amounts **(1)** and nuclear fallout from nuclear reactors **(1)** can be produced in major nuclear disasters **(1)**, from any radioactive waste produced in the reactor **(1)** and from the decommissioning process **(1)**.

54. Nuclear fission

1 Slow-moving neutrons **(1)** are absorbed by a nucleus **(1)** which becomes unstable and splits **(1)**.

2 A chain reaction is when many neutrons **(1)** are released from fission and go on to cause many more fission reactions **(1)**. A controlled chain reaction is when most neutrons are absorbed **(1)** and only one neutron per fission goes on to cause further fission **(1)**

3 (a) so that they are easily absorbed by nuclei/do not miss the nuclei **(1)** causing the nucleus to become unstable **(1)** OR so the nucleus will become unstable **(1)** and split, releasing thermal energy **(1)**. (b) any two of: so that the extra neutrons are absorbed as only one neutron per fission needs to go on to produce further fission **(1)** as otherwise the reaction would go out of control **(1)** leading to an explosion **(1)**

55. Nuclear power stations

1 (a) nuclear fuels do not release greenhouse gases which lead to global warming **(1)**, (b) nuclear fuels produce nuclear waste which is radioactive and can be dangerous to humans **(1)**

2 any four from: control rods absorb some of the neutrons **(1)** produced by the fission of uranium nuclei **(1)** so these neutrons cannot cause other uranium nuclei to fission **(1)**; if the control rods are pulled out of the core they will absorb fewer neutrons **(1)** so more fission reactions will happen **(1)** and more heat energy will be released **(1)**

56. Nuclear fusion

1 Two smaller nuclei **(1)** join together to form a more stable, heavier nucleus **(1)** and release energy as thermal energy **(1)**.

2 Fusion results in the joining of smaller nuclei **(1)** to form a nucleus with a slightly smaller mass; the leftover mass is converted to energy **(1)**. Fission results in the splitting of a larger nucleus to form more stable daughter nuclei of smaller mass **(1)**, with the small difference in mass being converted to energy **(1)**.

3 Fusion reactions only happen at very high temperatures and pressures, **(1)** it is very difficult to produce these conditions (for any length of time) **(1)** and currently more energy is needed to make the fusion reaction happen than it releases. **(1)**

57. Extended response – Radioactivity

*Answer could include the following points:

- Mention of plum pudding model with electrons inside a positive dough.
- Mention of Rutherford model with small, positive nucleus which is concentrated in a tiny space around which electrons orbit.
- Mention of Bohr model with electrons in defined energy shells.
- Mention of experimental methods for refining models (e.g. a description of how Rutherford's alpha particle experiment was conducted)
- Mention of evidence collected from experiments to show new, better models.
- Mention that evidence from experiments shows a better understanding and that this new knowledge replaces older knowledge since the new model is better.
- Mention that experiments need to be conducted to provide evidence based on calculations or theories that have been developed. Only when the experiment provides evidence for a new, better model is it accepted by the scientific community.

58. The Solar System

1 geocentric: Earth at centre, Sun and planets orbit the Earth **(1)**; heliocentric: Sun at centre, planets orbit the Sun **(1)**

2 Neptune, Uranus, Saturn, Jupiter, Mars, Earth, Venus, Mercury **(2 marks: all 8, 1 or 2 incorrect: 1 mark)**.

3 Greater distance **(1)** makes them dimmer **(1)**; recent developments in telescopes allow these to be seen **(1)**.

59. Satellites and orbits

1 Speed of a body in a circular orbit is constant **(1)** but velocity is changing as the direction of the body is constantly changing **(1)**.

2 Speed is greatest nearest the Sun **(1)** and velocity changes the most nearest the Sun **(1)** as direction changes most when nearest the Sun **(1)**. Velocity and speed are lower when further from the Sun **(1)**.

3 The orbital speed affects the radius of the orbit of the GPS satellite **(1)**. If its orbital speed increases it would move into an orbit of smaller radius **(1)** and if its orbital speed decreases it would move into an orbit of greater orbital radius **(1)**. The

speed of orbit is constant when a satellite is in an orbit of a fixed radius **(1)**.

60. Theories about the Universe

1 Steady state theory **(1)**, Big Bang theory **(1)**.

2 correct temperature **(1)** to suggest Universe started in a Big Bang **(1)** around 14 billion years ago **(1)**

3 (a) smallest red shift **(1)** as it is moving away from us at a lower speed **(1)**, (b) largest red shift **(1)** as it is moving away from us with the greatest speed **(1)**

61. Doppler effect and red-shift

1 (a) siren changing its frequency **(1)** as it moves relative to the observer, frequency greater on approach to observer and lower on recession from observer **(1)**, (b) red-shift of light waves/ spectral lines **(1)** for light from a galaxy or star that is moving away from us **(1)**

2 Absorption lines in the spectra of the light from the galaxy can be compared with the corresponding absorption lines of a stationary source **(1)**. The difference in the position/ wavelength/frequency **(1)** can be used to calculate the speed of the galaxy **(1)**.

62. Life cycle of stars

1 (a) gravitational attraction of dust and gas **(1)**, main-sequence star/hydrogen fusion **(1)**, red giant/expansion after hydrogen burning phase **(1)**, white dwarf/collapse **(1)**, (b) same as (a) until main sequence **(2)** followed by red supergiant and supernova explosion **(1)** followed by gravitational collapse to a neutron star for a massive star and to a black hole for a supermassive star **(1)**

2 The fate of a star depends on its mass **(1)**. Only high mass stars will become neutron stars or black holes **(1)**, and the Sun does not have enough mass to become one of these **(1)**.

3 Any four of: Gravity pulls dust and gas together to form the star when it has enough mass **(1)**, the forces are balanced **(1)** during the main sequence **(1)** stage of the star's life, thermal expansion will cause the star to expand/move off the main sequence **(1)** at the end of its hydrogen burning stage/when it becomes a red giant/supergiant **(1)**.

63. Observing the Universe

1 On Earth/Earth-based **(1)**, in space/above the Earth's atmosphere **(1)**.

2 Certain wavelengths of visible light can penetrate the Earth's atmosphere **(1)** so can be detected by Earth-based telescopes **(1)**. Other wavelengths of visible light are absorbed by the atmosphere **(1)** so cannot be detected on Earth and this requires telescopes to be placed above the Earth's atmosphere in space **(1)**.

3 greater magnification – see further **(1)**; record data digitally – gather more data **(1)**; greater precision – clearer images **(1)**; detect other electromagnetic waves instead of light – can observe other objects that emit other types of EM waves **(1)**

64. Extended response – Astronomy

*Answer could include the following points:

- Low-mass stars expand to become red giants after the main sequence.
- Low-mass stars that become red giants then become white dwarfs.
- High-mass stars become red supergiants after they move off the main sequence.
- High-mass red supergiant stars undergo supernova explosions.
- Remnant cores of supernovae can become neutron stars (1.4 to 3 solar masses).

- Most massive stars become black holes (greater mass than 3 solar masses).

65. Work, energy and power

1 work $= F \times d = 350\,\text{N} \times 30\,\text{m}$ **(1)** $= 1050$ **(1)** J **(1)**

2 energy $= P \times t = 1800\,\text{W} \times 8 \times 60\,\text{s}$ **(1)** $= 864\,000$ **(1)** J **(1)**

3 power $= E \div t = 3600\,\text{W} \div 60\,\text{s}$ **(1)** $= 60$ **(1)** W **(1)**

66. Extended response – Energy and forces

*Answer could include the following points:

- Refer to power as the rate of energy transfer (or similar).
- Refer to gain in gravitational potential energy as $mg\Delta h$ where Δh is the change in height masses are lifted.
- Δh is a control variable.
- Time measurement needed.
- Refer to the change in gravitational potential energy for both weightlifters over a period of time.
- Compare their power values using the equation: power = energy/time or $P = mg\Delta h/t$.
- Refer to the greater distance lifted per unit time is the most powerful weightlifter.
- Refer to keeping it a fair test – e.g. same masses for both weightlifters.

67. Interacting forces

1 Gravity is always an attractive force, whereas magnetism and the electrostatic force can be attractive or repulsive. **(1)**

2 Friction and drag always work to oppose motion/slow down a moving object. **(1)**

3 Contact forces are any two of: drag **(1)**, normal **(1)** and upthrust **(1)**. Non-contact force is the force of gravity acting on the ship **(1)**.

68. Moments

1 Moment = force × distance from pivot = 25 N × 2 m **(1)** = 50 **(1)** Nm **(1)**

2 Anticlockwise moments = clockwise moments **(1)** for a body that is balanced/in equilibrium, 30 N × 1 m = X N × 1.5 m **(1)**, 30 Nm = X N × 1.5 m **(1)**, X = 30/1.5 = 20 N **(1)**

69. Levers and gears

1 (a) seesaw or scissors **(1)**, (b) wheelbarrow **(1)**, (c) tweezers **(1)**

2 (a) a high gear is used for a higher speed **(1)** and a lower output turning force **(1)**, (b) a low gear is used at a low speed **(1)** to develop a higher output turning force **(1)**.

3 For a lever, a force at a distance on one side of the pivot in a clockwise direction **(1)** will lead to a turning effect/moment on the other side of the pivot in the anticlockwise direction – hence a rotation **(1)**. For a gear, if two gears are connected, the rotation of one gear in a clockwise direction **(1)** will lead to the connected gear to rotate in the anticlockwise direction **(1)**.

70. Extended response – Forces and their effects

*Answer could include the following points:

- Contact forces involve surfaces touching or being in contact.
- Non-contact forces involve bodies interacting at a distance and not being in contact.
- Examples of contact forces include friction, upthrust, reaction force.
- Examples of non-contact forces are gravitational force, magnetic force, electrostatic force.
- Contact forces such as reaction force and upthrust, if balanced, will cause a body to remain still or float.

- Contact forces, if balanced, can cause a body to move at a constant speed.
- Non-contact force of gravity will cause a body to accelerate towards Earth if there is a resultant force.
- Non-contact force of gravity will cause a body to move at a constant speed if the force of gravity is balanced by opposing frictional or drag force.
- Contact force of friction opposes the motion of a body and tries to slow it down.
- Other examples of balanced/unbalanced forces used as examples for magnetism or electrostatic force.

71. Circuit symbols

1 filament lamp **(1)**, motor **(1)**, LED **(1)**

2 ammeters in series **(1)**, voltmeters in parallel **(1)**

3 circuit to contain a cell **(1)**, lamp **(1)**, LDR **(1)**

72. Series and parallel circuits

1 Series: current same at all points **(1)**, potential differences across components add to give potential difference across cell **(1)**. Parallel: current splits at a junction **(1)**, potential difference across each branch is same as potential difference across cell **(1)**.

2 Current will stop flowing in series if one bulb breaks **(1)**, so parallel arrangement so that lights stay on **(1)** if one or more bulbs break **(1)**.

3 More bulbs in parallel means a higher current **(1)** is drawn from the cell, so finite amount of stored chemical energy **(1)** decreases **(1)** more rapidly **(1)**.

4 $A_1 = A_2 = 1\,A$ **(1)**, $V_1 = V_2 = 3\,V$ **(1)**

73. Current and charge

1 charge: coulomb **(1)**; current: ampere **(1)**

2 $Q = I \times t = 0.25\,A \times (60 \times 60)\,s$ **(1)** $= 900$ **(1)** C **(1)**

3 Charge = current × time, $3000\,C = 0.25\,A \times$ time **(1)**, time = $3000\,C \div 0.25\,A$ **(1)**, $= 12\,000$ **(1)** s **(1)**

74. Energy and charge

1 $E = Q \times V = 24\,C \times 6\,V$ **(1)** $= 144$ **(1)** J **(1)**

2 $V = E \div Q$ **(1)**, so since unit of energy is J and charge is C **(1)**, we get $1\,V = 1\,J/C$ **(1)**.

3 Energy = charge × potential difference, $400\,J = 50\,C \times V$ **(1)**, so $V = 400\,J \div 50\,C$, $= 8$ **(1)** V **(1)**

75. Ohm's law

1 $V = I \times R = 3.2\,A \times 18\,\Omega$ **(1)** $= 57.6$ **(1)** V **(1)**

2 $R = V \div I = 28\,V \div 0.4\,A$ **(1)** $= 70$ **(1)** Ω **(1)**

76. Resistors

$I = V \div R = 12\,V \div 120\,\Omega$ **(1)** $= 0.1$ **(1)** A **(1)**

77. I–V graphs

(a) graph of S-shaped curve through origin of I against V for filament lamp **(1)**, labelled axes **(1)**.

(b) As the current goes up, the temperature goes up **(1)** and as the temperature goes up the resistance goes up **(1)** and the gradient goes down **(1)**

78. Core practical – Electrical circuits

1 Current will flow through the components **(1)** in either arrangement, with the shape of the I–V graph being determined by the structure **(1)** of the component and whether it obeys Ohm's law or not **(1)**, not on how it is arranged in a circuit, since heat will still be dissipated in each circuit **(1)**.

2 As the p.d. increases across the filament lamp, the current through the filament lamp also increases **(1)** and as current increases, the energy is dissipated as heat increases leading to more vibrations of the metal ions in the filament **(1)**, which increases the resistance of the lamp **(1)** so the current increases by less and less per unit increase in p.d. **(1)** leading to a graph of decreasing gradient as the p.d. gets bigger and bigger **(1)**.

79. The LDR and the thermistor

1 (a) temperature **(1)**, (b) light intensity **(1)**

2 Provide an example of a circuit where temperature **(1)** and light intensity **(1)** vary their resistances **(1)** to turn on an output device **(1)**. The marks can only be awarded if the operation of the circuit is described in terms of changing light levels and temperature. An example would be for a circuit that turns a light/heater on or off in a greenhouse, for example.

80. Current heating effect

1 any three devices, e.g. oven, iron, heater, hair dryer, toaster, grill **(1 mark for each)**

2 Large current **(1)**, transfers much thermal energy **(1)** which may lead to a fire **(1)**.

3 The potential difference causes a current to flow **(1)**, the current causes the metal atoms to vibrate **(1)** the vibrations of the atoms cause thermal energy **(1)** to be dissipated **(1)**.

81. Energy and power

1 Power = current × potential difference, $= 13\,A \times 230\,V$ **(1)**, $= 2990$ **(1)** W **(1)**

2 Energy transferred = current × potential difference × time **(1)**, $= 1.5\,A \times 12\,V \times 120\,s$ **(1)**, $= 2160$ **(1)** J **(1)**

82. A.c. and d.c. circuits

1 (a) any three devices, e.g. remote controls, torches, mobile phones, calculators, watches, etc. **(1 mark each)**. (b) any three mains-operated devices, e.g. electric oven, microwave oven, fridge, freezer, tumble dryer, hairdryer, TV, etc. **(1 mark each)**

2 (a) They both transfer energy **(1)**. (b) Potential difference in a.c. alternates **(1)** but in d.c. it is constant **(1)**.

3 Energy transferred = power × time **(1)**. The power rating of the electric oven is 200 times bigger than that of the electric shaver **(1)**. So the energy transferred (in the same amount of time) will be 200 times bigger for the oven than the shaver **(1)**.

83. Mains electricity and the plug

1 (a) brown **(1)** (b) blue **(1)** (c) yellow and green **(1)**

2 advantage of fuse: cheaper **(1)**; advantage of circuit breaker – one of: more sensitive to current **(1)**, does not need to be replaced (reset by pressing a switch) **(1)**, more reliable **(1)**, responds faster **(1)**

3 Live wire touches metal case **(1)**, earth wire forms circuit with live wire and pulls a large current through the fuse **(1)**, large current melts fuse and isolates appliance **(1)**, device now at $0\,V$ and no longer dangerous to user **(1)**.

84. Extended response – Electricity and circuits

*Answer could include the following points:

- Fuse will melt if the current entering an appliance is too big.
- Earth wire pulls a large current through a fuse and melts the fuse wire if the live wire comes into contact with the metal casing.
- Mention that fuse/earth wire are safety devices.
- Mention fuse is connected to live wire so that device will be at $0\,V$ when the fuse blows.

- Fuse/earth wire isolate the appliance so that device case cannot become live and so protects the user from the electrocution/ fires occurring due to overheating.
- The fuse rating should be close to, but above, the current taken by the appliance so as to avoid any risk of the device overheating/catching fire due to the current becoming too high and producing too much thermal energy.

85. Static electricity

1 (a) negatively charged **(1)**, (b) positively charged **(1)**
2 **B** positive duster and negative rod **(1)**
3 Protons are held in the nucleus **(1)** by strong forces **(1)** so too much energy would be required **(1)** to transfer them.
4 Polythene is rubbed and becomes negatively charged **(1)** as it gains electrons; opposite charges attract **(1)**, so suspended rod will move towards the polythene **(1)** if positively charged.

86. Electrostatic phenomena

1 Plastic is an insulator and will keep any electrons that are rubbed onto it **(1)**; metal is a conductor so isolated electrons will not stay on it **(1)**.
2 Friction **(1)** between the carpet and shoes causes electrons **(1)** to move onto your shoes which are insulators **(1)**. These are earthed when a conductor is touched **(1)**. The current caused by the movement of the electrons causes the shock **(1)**.
3 Clouds become charged due to electrons being transferred between ice particles by friction **(1)** so one part of each cloud is positive and one part is negative **(1)** and a potential difference is set up between the opposite charges on each cloud **(1)** so there will be a discharge of electrons as lightning **(1)**.

87. Electrostatics uses and dangers

1 The spray droplets gain electrons when they pass through the nozzle **(1)** and these all have the same charge, causing the droplets to repel and spread out **(1)**.
2 The nozzle of the sprayer is connected to an electrical supply/ potential difference **(1)**. As droplets of insecticide pass through the nozzle they will either lose or gain electrons and so all have the same charge **(1)** causing them to repel each other **(1)** leading to a fine spray **(1)** that covers a large area of the plants.
3 Friction of plane with air meaning it can become charged **(1)**, which could ignite fuel **(1)** and cause an explosion **(1)**

88. Electric fields

1 (a) Greater mass means less acceleration **(1)** from $a = F/m$ **(1)**.
   (b) It would move in the opposite direction **(1)** with the same initial acceleration **(1)**.
2 An electric field is created in the region around a charged particle **(1)**. If another charged particle is placed in (the region of) this electric field then it will experience a non-contact force **(1)** which will cause it to be attracted or repelled **(1)**. Electrons (negatively charged) are attracted to the positive charge which explains the phenomenon of static electricity **(1)**.

89. Extended response – Static electricity

*Answer could include the following points:
- Insulators can be charged if rubbed with a cloth, for example.
- Conductors cannot remain charged if rubbed.
- Electrons will move onto or off the insulator.
- Materials become negatively charged if electrons are gained or positively charged if they lose electrons.
- Refer to electrostatic induction/charge at surface of one material inducing opposite charge at the surface of the other (e.g. the tissue paper).
- Refer to attraction due to opposite charges close to each other.

- Refer to this happening for materials where induction can occur in insulators or metals by providing a suitable example.

90. Magnets and magnetic fields

1 (a) similar to the diagram for the bar magnet **(1)** but with fewer field lines **(1)**; (b) similar to the diagram for the uniform field **(1)** but with more field lines **(1)**
2 The permanent magnet always induces **(1)** the opposite pole **(1)** next to its pole causing it to attract **(1)**.
3 A permanent magnet has N and S poles all of the time **(1)**, a temporary magnet is a magnetic material that does not have magnetic poles **(1)** but can be magnetised/attracted when placed near a permanent magnet **(1)**.

91. Current and magnetism

1 similar to diagram on page 91 **(1)**, but with the arrows in the opposite direction **(1)**
2 Current doubles so field doubles **(1)**, distance doubles so field halves **(1)**, so overall there is no change **(1)**.
3 Increase the size of the current flowing **(1)**, increase the number of turns of wire per metre on the coil **(1)**, insert a magnetic material as the core **(1)**.

92. Extended response – Magnetism and the motor effect

*Answer could include the following points:
- The closer a magnet is to an object, the stronger the magnetic field that it will experience, so the greater the mass it can attract.
- A greater electric current will cause the strength of the magnetic field around an electromagnet to be greater.
- More turns on the coil or a coiled wire instead of a straight wire increases the strength of the magnetic field from the electromagnetic field, so a greater mass can be picked up or attracted.
- Using a soft iron core will increase the strength of the magnetic field around a solenoid/electromagnet so more mass can be attracted.
- Mention that certain materials where magnetism can be induced will be attracted, whereas others will not – iron, cobalt, nickel, steel will be, but others will not be.
- Mention that certain materials that are themselves permanent magnets will be attracted based on their magnetic field strengths, even when no current flows through an electromagnet.

93. Transformers

1 The amount of electrical energy transferred by heating in the National Grid is related to the size of the current **(1)**, so with a small current, energy transferred by heating is reduced **(1)** which increases the efficiency of the system **(1)**.
2 $V_p \times I_p = V_s \times I_s$, 24 V $\times I_p$ = 120 V $\times$ 0.5 A **(1)**, I_p = 120 V $\times$ 0.5 A $\div$ 24 V **(1)** = 5 **(1)** A **(1)**

94. Extended response – Electromagnetic induction

*Answer could include the following points:
- Transformer has primary and secondary coil and works with a.c. input only.
- The current is stepped down when the voltage is stepped up to conserve power and not violate the principle of conservation of energy.
- Voltage is stepped up by transformers when it leaves the power station for transmission across the UK on wires.

- Voltage is stepped down to safer levels when electricity is supplied to homes, hospitals and factories.
- Current is low as power loss is minimised with a lower current: power loss is proportional to the current squared, $P \propto I^2$.
- Lower current means thinner wires means less expensive to buy means lower cost to the consumer.

95. Changes of state

1 Thermal energy is transferred from the warmer room to the ice **(1)** and causes the ice to melt **(1)** and become 1.5 kg of liquid water **(1)**.

2 As the gas cools, the particles slow down and occupy a smaller volume **(1)** and make fewer collisions with the container they are in **(1)** so the pressure decreases too **(1)**.

3 Thermal energy is supplied to the copper metal, bonds are broken and it turns from a solid to a liquid at a constant temperature **(1)** once it reaches its melting point **(1)**. Further heating of the liquid copper causes its temperature **(1)** to rise until it reaches its boiling point, at which point it turns from a liquid to a gas at a constant temperature **(1)**. If the gaseous copper atoms continue to be heated then the temperature of the gas will increase **(1)**.

96. Density

1 density = mass ÷ volume = 862 g ÷ 765 cm³ **(1)** = 1.1 **(1)** g/cm³ **(1)**

2 50 000 cm³ = 5000 ÷ 1 000 000 m³ = 0.05 m³ **(1)**, mass = density × volume = 0.05 m³ × 2700 kg/m³ **(1)** = 135 **(1)** kg **(1)**

97. Core practical – Investigating density

1 density = mass ÷ volume = 454 g ÷ 256 cm³ **(1)** = 1.77 **(1)** g/cm³ **(1)**

2 Mass reading can be misread by human error or by parallax error or by systematic error **(1)**; volume can be misread by parallax error or reading the top of the meniscus for water **(1)**; a value that is too high for the mass **(1)** or too low for the volume will lead to a value that is too high for the density **(1)**.

98. Energy and changes of state

1 ΔQ = 15 kg × 4200 J/kg °C × (74 °C – 18 °C) **(1)** = 3 528 000 **(1)** J **(1)**

2 Energy supplied = specific latent heat of melting of water × mass of water, = 334 000 J/kg × 20 kg **(1)**, = 6 680 000 **(1)** J **(1)**

99. Core practical – Thermal properties of water

1 Less thermal energy is lost to the surroundings **(1)** and more is used to heat the water **(1)** so the value obtained is closer to the true value required to cause a temperature change of 1 °C for that mass of liquid **(1)**; alternatively, state that losing more to the surroundings **(1)** requires more energy than necessary to be supplied for unit temperature change **(1)** of unit mass **(1)**.

2 (a) When water is heated in liquid form/the same state of matter **(1)** such as when water is being heated in a pan or being boiled in a kettle **(1)**, (b) when it is changing state **(1)** e.g. when it is melting or boiling **(1)**.

3 Diagram should show ice in a funnel over a beaker, with an electric heater in the ice **(1)** and a thermometer (which should be away from the heater) **(1)** and a stopwatch **(1)**.

100. Pressure and temperature

1 (a) 20 + 273 = 293 K **(1)**
(b) 300 – 273 = 27 °C **(1)**

2 The kinetic energy of a gas is directly proportional to the temperature **(1)** of the gas in kelvin **(1)** so doubling the temperature doubles the average kinetic energy of the molecules in the gas **(1)**.

3 (a) The average speed is slower **(1)**. (b) The pressure is reduced **(1)** because there are fewer collisions/the particles do not hit the walls as hard **(1)**.

101. Volume and pressure

1 The volume of the gas will decrease **(1)**, the molecules will get closer together **(1)** and collide more often with the walls of the container **(1)**.

2 $P_2 = P_1 \times V_1 \div V_2$ **(1)** 200 000 Pa × 28 cm³ ÷ 44.8 cm³ **(1)** = 125 000 Pa (or 125 kPa) **(1)**

3 (a) A gas compressed slowly **(1)** will change volume at a constant temperature as the thermal energy from the compression will be able to leave the system **(1)**. (b) A quick compression of a gas **(1)** means that work is done on the gas but in a tiny time period so that the increase in energy is the extra kinetic energy of the particles of gas **(1)**.

102. Extended response – Density

*Answer could include the following points:
- Pressure is caused by moving particles colliding with the sides of a container.
- Pressure is force per unit area.
- Decreasing the volume of a gas quickly means that work is being done on the gas.
- When work is done on the gas the kinetic energy/speed of the particles increases.
- Faster moving particles collide with the walls/area more frequently, leading to an increase in pressure.
- Increasing the temperature of a gas at constant volume means that the particles have greater kinetic energy and speed and so collide more frequently with the area, so greater pressure.
- The internal energy of a gas is entirely kinetic.

103. Elastic and inelastic distortion

1 (a) two equal forces **(1)** of tension acting in opposite directions **(1)**, (b) two equal forces **(1)** acting towards one another **(1)**

2 (a) any two suitable examples, e.g. springs **(1)**, elastic bands **(1)**, rubber **(1)**, skin **(1)**, (b) any two suitable examples, e.g. springs beyond elastic limit **(1)**, putty **(1)**, Plasticine **(1)**, bread dough **(1)**, wet chewing gum **(1)**

3 It will not return to its original shape **(1)** when the force is removed **(1)** and will be longer than it was originally/extended **(1)**.

104. Springs

1 (a) Force = spring constant × extension, = 30 N/m × 0.2 m **(1)**, = 6 **(1)** N **(1)**

(b) Work done = energy stored = $\frac{1}{2}$ × spring constant × extension², = $\frac{1}{2}$ × 30 N/m × (0.2 m)² **(1)**, = 0.6 **(1)** J **(1)**

2 The greater the value of the spring constant **(1)**, the greater the force is needed **(1)** to extend the spring by the same amount/by 1 m **(1)**.

3 10 cm = 0.1 m **(1)**, energy stored = $\frac{1}{2}$ × spring constant × extension², = $\frac{1}{2}$ × 45 N/m × (0.1 m)² **(1)**, = 0.225 **(1)** J **(1)**

105 Core practical – Forces and springs

1 energy stored = $\frac{1}{2}kx^2$ = $\frac{1}{2}$ × 5 N/m × (0.5 m)² **(1)** = 0.625 **(1)** J **(1)**

2 Yes; a force has been applied to *decrease* the length of the spring which still means that elastic potential energy is stored in the spring/work has been done on the spring when it is being compressed **(1)**.

The spring constant can be calculated from the gradient of a force/compression graph or a force/extension graph **(1)**.

The energy stored in the spring can be found from the area beneath a force/compression or force/extension graph **(1)**.

106. Pressure

1 Pressure = force ÷ area = $600\,N \div 2.5\,m^2$ **(1)** = 240 **(1)** Pa or N/m^2 **(1)**

2 Total pressure affected by depth **(1)**, density of the liquid/gas **(1)** and atmospheric pressure **(1)**

107. Extended response – Forces and matter

*Answer could include the following points:

- Distortion is when a force causes a body to extend or change shape.

- The extension is directly proportional to the load/force applied for elastic distortion.

- The body/spring/material will return to its original shape when the force/load is removed.

- Inelastic distortion is when the body is extended beyond its elastic limit.

- The body will then not return to its original shape but will remain permanently extended.

- The spring constant for a spring is found from the gradient of the force–extension graph provided that the linear region only is used.

- The spring constant may be found from $k = F \div x$.

- Energy stored is found from $E = \frac{1}{2}kx^2$ or from the area beneath the line.

Physics Equations List

In your exam, you will be provided with the following list of equations. Make sure you are clear which equations will be given to you in the exam. You will need to learn the equations that aren't on the equations list.

Equations

(final velocity)^2 – (initial velocity)^2 = 2 × acceleration × distance $v^2 - u^2 = 2 \times a \times x$
energy transferred = current × potential difference × time $E = I \times V \times t$
potential difference across primary coil × current in primary coil $\qquad\qquad\qquad$ = potential difference across secondary coil × current in secondary coil $V_p \times I_p = V_s \times I_s$
change in thermal energy = mass × specific heat capacity × change in temperature $\Delta Q = m \times c \times \Delta\theta$
thermal energy for a change of state = mass × specific latent heat $Q = m \times L$
$P_1 V_1 = P_2 V_2$ to calculate pressure or volume for gases of fixed mass at constant temperature
energy transferred in stretching = 0.5 × spring constant × (extension)^2 $E = \frac{1}{2} \times k \times x^2$

Your own notes

Your own notes

Your own notes

Your own notes

Your own notes

Your own notes

Your own notes

Published by Pearson Education Limited, 80 Strand, London, WC2R 0RL.

www.pearsonschoolsandfecolleges.co.uk

Copies of official specifications for all Edexcel qualifications may be found on the website: www.edexcel.com

Text © Pearson Education Limited 2017
Typeset and produced by Phoenix Photosetting
Illustrated by TechSet Ltd.
Cover illustration by Miriam Sturdee

The right of Dr Mike O'Neill to be identified as author of this work has been asserted by him in accordance with the Copyright, Designs and Patents Act 1988.

First published 2017

24
10 9 8 7 6

British Library Cataloguing in Publication Data
A catalogue record for this book is available from the British Library

ISBN 978 1 292 13369 0

Printed in Great Britain by Bell and Bain Ltd, Glasgow

Acknowledgements
Content written by Penny Johnson and Steve Woolley is included.

The author and publisher would like to thank the following organisations for permission to reproduce copyright material:

Maps
Map on page 43 adapted from https://www.gov.uk/government/organisations/health-protection-agency, Radon Affected Areas in England and Wales – Health Protection Agency. Esri, HERE, DeLorme, FAO, NOAA, USGS. © Crown copyright. Contains public sector information licensed under the Open Government Licence (OGL) v3.0. http://www.nationalarchives.gov.uk/doc/open-government-licence/version/3/

Figures
Figure on page 18 adapted from *Energy Transitions: History, Requirements, Prospects*, Praeger (Vaclav Smil 2010), BP Statistical Review of World Energy 2016

All other images © Pearson Education

A note from the publisher
In order to ensure that this resource offers high-quality support for the associated Pearson qualification, it has been through a review process by the awarding body. This process confirms that this resource fully covers the teaching and learning content of the specification or part of a specification at which it is aimed. It also confirms that it demonstrates an appropriate balance between the development of subject skills, knowledge and understanding, in addition to preparation for assessment.

Endorsement does not cover any guidance on assessment activities or processes (e.g. practice questions or advice on how to answer assessment questions), included in the resource nor does it prescribe any particular approach to the teaching or delivery of a related course.

While the publishers have made every attempt to ensure that advice on the qualification and its assessment is accurate, the official specification and associated assessment guidance materials are the only authoritative source of information and should always be referred to for definitive guidance.

Pearson examiners have not contributed to any sections in this resource relevant to examination papers for which they have responsibility.

Examiners will not use endorsed resources as a source of material for any assessment set by Pearson.

Endorsement of a resource does not mean that the resource is required to achieve this Pearson qualification, nor does it mean that it is the only suitable material available to support the qualification, and any resource lists produced by the awarding body shall include this and other appropriate resources.